Rejected, Shamed, and Blamed

REJECTED, SHAMED, AND BLAMED

Help and Hope for Adults in the Family Scapegoat Role

By Rebecca C. Mandeville MFT

First digital edition: August 2020 (revised September 2021)

ISBN: 9781393229773 (Kindle eBook version)

Author Website: scapegoatrecovery.com

Disclaimer: This digital publication is not intended as a substitute for the medical advice of professionals. The reader should consult a physician or licensed mental health professional in matters relating to their health, particularly concerning any symptoms that may require diagnosis or medical attention. When it comes to practical advice books and/or guides, readers are cautioned and expected to rely on their own judgment about their circumstances and act accordingly. Although the author has made every effort to ensure that the information in this book was correct at the time of publication, she does not assume and hereby disclaims any liability to any party for any loss, damage, or disruption caused by errors or omissions, whether such errors or omissions result from negligence, accident, or any other cause. Adherence to all applicable laws and regulations, including international, federal, state, and local governing professional licensing, business practices, advertising, and all other aspects of doing business in the US, Canada, or any other jurisdiction is the sole responsibility of the reader and consumer. Any perceived slight of any individual or organization is purely unintentional.

Contents

This work is dedicated to my clients, past and present. Your sincere and earnest commitment to uncovering and reclaiming the totality of your Being inspires me daily.

Foreword

This much-needed work by *Rebecca C. Mandeville* provides a comprehensive introduction to the subject of *Family Scapegoating* and serves as a starting point for survivor awareness and further research for professionals if they want to begin filling in the gaps for this misunderstood and underserved community. It is dense and informative, but with a writing style that makes it easy to read. I found myself re-reading paragraphs that had flowed by to capture Rebecca's insights and innovative nomenclature, which are too profound to breeze through. Because it lacks fluff and stories, it serves as both a reference and a guide that includes relevant resources and recovery recommendations.

The scapegoat role has always been with us, but the phenomenon has not been adequately or directly addressed within *Mental Health* literature. For this reason, many adults in the family scapegoat role have great difficulty getting a proper diagnosis (which is often complex PTSD, as addressed in this book), as well as difficulty finding adequate support and therapy. Family systems information can help, but the additional layers of grief cannot be addressed or fully healed without greater understanding.

This book also serves an important niche within *Family Systems* literature, as it was written for those who were assigned the role of family scapegoat within their dysfunctional family system. It adeptly addresses with specificity the abuses and emotional injuries scapegoated adults experience, which are distinct, and often more damaging than those associated with other dysfunctional family roles. The author tackles a difficult, little-understood subject with a great measure of compassion and professionalism.

Lisa Marie Campagnoli, CRTC, RYT-200

Certified Trauma Recovery Coach and Founder of Lifelandscape Coach, LLC

Introduction

"I could not ask for forgiveness for something I had not done. As scapegoat, I could only bear the fault."

— Daphne du Maurier, *The Scapegoat* (Novel)

Note From the Author: This **introductory guide** was created in response to requests from readers of my international blog on dysfunctional family systems and scapegoating, a blog that was originally created for the popular online Mental Health resource center, *Psych Central.*

This guide's purpose is to increase insight and understanding regarding the painful reality experienced by those who suffer from a particularly insidious form of psycho-emotional abuse within their family-of-origin. It is informed by over two decades of my working with adult survivors who are in the 'scapegoat' or 'identified patient' role within their dysfunctional family system, and by research I conducted while serving as Core Faculty at the *Institute of Transpersonal Psychology* (now known as *Sofia University*) on what I named *family scapegoating abuse (FSA).*

While this is not a 'recovery workbook', by examining the

experiences and symptoms common to the FSA adult survivor; FSA's relationship with **complex trauma (C-PTSD)**; and the importance of engaging in **trauma-informed recovery approaches**, I hope to offer support, validation, education, and resources to those who find themselves trapped in the painful 'family scapegoat' role.

To learn more about family scapegoating abuse (FSA) or to subscribe to my newsletter or blog, visit *scapegoatrecovery.com.*

———————————

Were you chronically bullied, shamed, blamed, or rejected by a parent, sibling, or other relative while growing up? Have you ever been the target of an intentionally malicious 'smear' campaign perpetrated by immediate or extended family members and been left feeling frustrated, angry, helpless, or confused? Perhaps you've been called "crazy," a "liar," or "a fake" by your own mother, father, or siblings and have no idea why they are speaking about you in this way.

Desperate to understand what has been happening to you within your family-of-origin, you may have reached out to a friend, minister, or Mental Health professional and been told, "You need to find a way to get over it, it's your family, it can't be that bad". Unsure of how to adequately describe what you've been experiencing. you may feel discouraged, hopeless, and alone, deprived of emotional understanding and appropriate concern and support.

My name is Rebecca C. Mandeville and I'm a licensed

Marriage and Family Therapist. As a *Psychotherapist, Recovery Coach, Educator,* and recognized *Family Systems* expert specializing in child and adult psycho-emotional abuse (aka 'hidden' or 'invisible' abuse), I've spent over two decades helping people both understand and recover from the mental and emotional damage caused by growing up in dysfunctional, 'toxic' family systems. My experience in counseling and coaching adult survivors of family scapegoating and my qualitative research on what I named *family scapegoating abuse (FSA)* now inform this work.

In these pages you'll discover:

- How to **recognize** and **identify** family scapegoating abuse (FSA) **signs and symptoms**

- Why scapegoated individuals have difficulty recognizing they are being **abused**

- How **complex trauma (C-PTSD), betrayal trauma,** and **toxic shame** impede FSA recovery

- How **intergenerational trauma** and **false narratives** contribute to family scapegoating dynamics

- Why the **family 'Empath'** can end up scapegoated

- Steps to reduce **fawning behaviors** and recover and realign with your 'true self'

If you've been scapegoated by your family (particularly if the scapegoating began when you were very young and is chronic), you may be suffering from a variety of life challenges and mental health symptoms, including relationship issues; impostor syndrome; generalized anxiety; depression; addiction; codependency; and complex trauma symptoms.

You may have no idea that your psycho-emotional distress is due to your being trapped in the role of *'identified patient'* in your family. Alternatively, you may know you are in the 'scapegoat' role but you're not sure how to change these dysfunctional family dynamics so you can be seen for who you actually are.

Many readers of my articles on family scapegoating have written to me to express the intensity of emotions they experience when recognizing themselves as family scapegoating abuse survivors. Typical comments include, "I didn't know there was a name for what I've gone through – it's like you're writing about my life!" Also, "Now that I understand what may have happened to me, I have hope that perhaps there's a way for me to recover." Once a lovely woman in her eighties wrote to me to say, "Thank you for helping me to understand what I've been experiencing for most of my life. I can now live the rest of my life with some peace, however long that is."

My understanding of family scapegoating and its damaging effects is based on countless hours spent working with both individuals and families in residential treatment settings and in my psychotherapy and coaching practices, as well as my qualitative research on family scapegoating dynamics and how the targeted child or adult child is negatively impacted.

This guide is also informed by my own experiences of being in the 'family scapegoat' role myself – a role 'inherited' from my mother, who shared with me that she was severely scapegoated by a grandmother in early childhood during a revealing conversation we once had.

I have also benefited from reading personal messages and comments in response to my articles and social media posts on family scapegoating abuse (FSA). These painful and honest sharings from hundreds of people around the world have also illuminated this work.

The Intergenerational Aspects of FSA

Recovering from family scapegoating requires recognizing that being the 'identified patient' is symptomatic of generations of systemic dysfunction within one's family, fueled by unrecognized anxiety and intergenerational trauma. In a certain sense, members of a dysfunctional family are participating in a *consensual trance,* i.e., a 'survival trance' supported by false narratives, toxic shame, anxiety, and *egoic defense mechanisms,* such as *denial* and *projection.*

It was not until I did my *family genogram* as part of my *Masters in Counseling Psychology* training that I learned of some of the devastating, traumatic events that had impacted my family-of-origin. Similarly, many of the genograms my clients have done as part of their family systems exploration reveal sudden, unexpected deaths (including suicides); severe or chronic illness; stillbirths; mental illness (including institutionalization of a parent or other close relative); divorce; abandonment; addiction; overt or covert abuse (including abuse of children); missing relatives; emotional cut-offs; and profound financial setbacks and losses.

The resulting patterns, behaviors, and family roles that are transmitted from generation-to-generation due to the underlying anxiety and trauma associated with adverse experiences and events form a 'matrix', of sorts, one that acts like an energetic spider web that is seemingly impossible for the child or adult child to resist, challenge, or escape from.

For those who do 'wake up' and realize that there is another reality outside the one they were inoculated into since infancy within their family-of-origin, it can be a bit of a shock – similar to Keanu Reeves' experience in the 1999 film 'The Matrix' after he was ejected from the dystopian simulated reality he had unknowingly been existing within. The truth, once uncovered, cannot be forgotten about or ignored. And truth can act as a destabilizing force in families that depend on false narratives, control, and denial to maintain their equilibrium.

The Abusive Aspects of Family Scapegoating

While disagreements and interpersonal conflicts are common in even the healthiest of family systems, family scapegoating goes far beyond this, making recovering from its impact and effects difficult. For example, more than half of those who responded to an *FSA Survey* I conducted have been described as "mentally ill"; "emotionally sick"; or "a liar" by a parent, sibling, or other close relative when there was absolutely no truth to this whatsoever. Naturally, being spoken about in this way can be confusing, angering, and traumatizing to the target of such hostile and defamatory statements.

It should also be noted that a more recent FSA research study I conducted confirmed that family scapegoating can begin in adulthood, often initiated by a divorce or a change in financial circumstances. For example, many of my clients who became a target of FSA as adults report that the family scapegoating began when they were divorcing a spouse. "My own family supported my ex and not me!" is a refrain I often hear, particularly in cases where the ex-spouse was influential in the family, financially well-off, or highly narcissistic and charismatic. Other clients have shared that the scapegoating they experienced in their family became severe when they became successful or were positively recognized by others in some manner. Is it any wonder such clients feel confused and deeply betrayed by the people they counted on to be there for them the most during a time of great accomplishment, crisis, or need?

In addition to the challenges related to dis-identifying from the family 'scapegoat narrative' and attendant distorted stories and gossip, it has been my experience clinically that many FSA adult survivors are suffering from symptoms of undiagnosed, untreated *Complex post-traumatic stress disorder (C-PTSD)* as well as *betrayal trauma* (which I discuss in more detail in this guide). Thus, **trauma is an area that must also be addressed if one is to fully recover from the negative effects of being scapegoated by their family** (an issue that I'll be covering in this guide).

A final point: While being scapegoated within one's family-of-origin is recognized as being harmful, the damage done is most often categorized as mental and emotional. However, being in the role of the *family scapegoat* can also result in the targeted child being physically bullied, sexually abused, or denied medical care – a sad reality that often goes unnoticed and unaddressed.

How to Use This Guide

Because reading about any form of family dysfunction or relational abuse can be intense and possibly triggering (especially for those who suffer from complex trauma symptoms), it is my suggestion that you be in an environment that feels calming and emotionally safe while reading this guide.

You may also want to take breaks after reading each chapter or after completing the included *FSA Self-Assessment* to do some reflection and journaling, or share your thoughts or any feelings that come up with your therapist, coach, or a trusted friend.

Lastly, **FSA recovery suggestions and resources** are listed throughout this book. Terms and concepts that you might wish to explore further are **italicized** where applicable. Healing modalities that work well for *FSA Recovery* can be found in the 'Unique Challenges of FSA Recovery' chapter. **Additional recovery recommendations** can be found in this guide's '**Afterword**' and '**Resources**' sections.

1

THE INVISIBLE WOUNDS OF THE SCAPEGOAT CHILD

Are you wondering if you're trapped in the painful, dysfunctional 'family scapegoat' role? Do you come from a dysfunctional (alcoholic/ toxic/abusive) family system and are experiencing difficulty finding adequate support and appropriate resources to help guide you in your healing and recovery process?

Recognizing Family Scapegoating Abuse (FSA)

If you're in the 'family scapegoat' role, you may have felt rejected or bullied by a parent, sibling, cousin, or in-law and are unable to comprehend how you became the target of their hostility and maltreatment.

You may have been devastated by a family 'smear' campaign (i.e., one or more family members seek to defame your character or damage your reputation by spreading negative or false propaganda to others about you) but few people, even some of your closest friends, can understand why you're so frustrated, angry, or distressed.

You may struggle to find competent professionals (doctors, therapists, counselors, coaches) who understand how genuinely emotionally debilitating it is to be the focus of negative, 'shaming and blaming' narratives within your family-of-origin or extended family.

***

In Murray Bowen's *Family Systems* theory, families are viewed as emotionally interrelated systems. Scapegoating in a dysfunctional family system is therefore viewed as being a manifestation of unconscious processes whereby the family displaces their collective psychological difficulties and complexes onto a specific family member.

Unacknowledged feelings such as guilt, frustration, shame, and anger are redirected onto the most vulnerable member of the group (often the youngest child, but not always). In this way, the scapegoated child is subjected to rejecting, shaming, and blaming behaviors via what is known as a *Family Projection Process* (which I will expand upon later).

While some family scapegoating processes may indeed be unconscious, the scapegoating of a family member can be conscious, intentional, and deliberate in cases where the scapegoating is driven by someone who is narcissistic or has narcissistic traits (such as lack of empathy and insight) or is otherwise personality disordered, mentally ill, or is a sociopath or sadistic.

Scapegoating can also occur when the child was a victim of sexual abuse and the perpetrator (a family member or someone connected to the family) wants to discredit the child or adult child so that they are not viewed as a believable reporter were they to tell someone about the abuse.

The Insidious Nature of Family Scapegoating

Children who are scapegoated in families are in reality victims of abuse and neglect, yet this is rarely recognized within our Mental Health, Family Court, or Educational systems. Because scapegoating processes can be subtle, many scapegoated adult survivors fail to realize that they have suffered from psycho-emotional abuse growing up, and even their therapist or counselor might miss the signs and symptoms associated with being in this most difficult dysfunctional family role.

Specifically: Adults seeking assistance from a mental health professional may find that the genuine pain and distress they are experiencing is minimized, dismissed, or invalidated (e.g., "But they're your family, of *course* they love you"; "Family connections are so important, it can't be that bad"; "It's best if you forgive, we need to maintain ties with our family to be healthy"), which only serves to reinforce the scapegoated adult's sense of confusion and isolation.

Scapegoating Is a Process of Dehumanization

While most people might occasionally feel excluded or 'left out' of their family for one reason or another, family scapegoating behaviors go far beyond that. In fact, scapegoating is closely related to bullying, and both qualify as overt or covert forms of psycho-emotional abuse. As with bullying, the scapegoated child can be subjected to aggressive domination and intimidation tactics, replete with threats, use of force, or coercion, with no means of escape.

Common statements from parents that scapegoat include, "Janie has emotional problems, she was such a difficult baby, but I did the best I could with her," or "Johnny is a liar, you can't believe anything he says, he's just like his father that way." The scapegoated child is repeatedly cast into a negative light and portrayed in a one-dimensional manner that denies them their full humanity, with all of the attendant negative and harmful consequences.

Why would a parent reject, shame, blame, and seek to dominate their own child? One primary reason is that the parent may suffer from unrecognized, untreated trauma. Another is that they may have *Borderline Personality Disorder* or *Narcissistic Personality Disorder* causing them to be highly aggressive, dominating, or unstable. They may have an undiagnosed, untreated Axis I condition such as *Bipolar Disorder* or an *Anxiety Disorder* or *Major Depressive Disorder,* causing them to attack their child to release their pent up frustrations and deep feelings of abandonment, 'toxic shame', or self-hatred.

Such parents (*Borderline*-types, especially) might engage in 'splitting' behaviors as well, e.g., they might pit one sibling against the other to create a camp of 'allies'. Parents that 'split' will also tend to see one child as 'good' (the 'golden child') and another as 'bad' (the 'scapegoat'). The role of 'scapegoat' in particular is not static and may shift from child to child or to a parent, particularly when one of the parents is mentally ill or an active addict/alcoholic.

Whatever the scenario, the scapegoated child is invariably portrayed as faulty and defective, deserving of the family's hostility and unworthy of love and inclusion. The rejected and shamed child is repeatedly objectified, dehumanized, and ostracized, becoming little more than a 'human movie screen' that is the recipient of the family's unconscious projections. I have heard many accounts from clients who have suffered in this manner, and their stories of negligence and abuse (including physical and sexual) are heartbreaking.

The Narcissistic Family System and Scapegoating

When a child is scapegoated within a *narcissistic family system*, that chronic maltreatment can be particularly acute. This is because the narcissistic parent governing such a system requires that their children and spouse idolize and revere them, similar to how a cult leader insists on their group members adoring them and complying with their wishes.

Children in such families are nothing more than mirrors whose sole purpose is to reflect back to the narcissistic parent their own (imagined) perfect and faultless image. The child that mirrors the parent in gratifying ways will inhabit the role of *golden child* (the 'perfect' child that can do no wrong), while the *scapegoat child* carries the tremendous burden of the narcissistic parent's repressed, unconscious self-hatred, including the 'shadow' parts of their psyche that they cannot consciously acknowledge or 'own'.

Family Scapegoating Is Psycho-Emotional Abuse

It was not until recently that *family scapegoating* began to be recognized as a form of systemic bullying and abuse within the Mental Health field. This is likely because family scapegoating is insidious in that it is supported by power discrepancies within the dysfunctional family system, i.e., the scapegoating parent's stories about the child are believed while the scapegoated child's reality and experiences are dismissed.

This is also the case when the child becomes an adult and attempts to share their negative, wounding family experiences with others. It is quite common for adult survivors of child psycho-emotional abuse to be told by those they confide in to stop being the "victim" and get over their childhood and "learn to forgive." I've had clients tell me that they have heard this same suggestion from previous therapists, which caused them to feel a profound sense of inferiority, guilt, and shame.

The Damaging Scapegoat Narrative

The scapegoating parent (who is typically the 'power-holder' in the family system, and therefore in control of the family narrative) often has a 'story' about their child that they are quick to share with anyone who will listen – a story whereby they are 'good' and their (scapegoated) child is "difficult," a "problem," "bad," and somehow innately defective. This distorted narrative designed to elevate the parent and demean the child is shared within and outside of the family, resulting in siblings, extended relatives, and friends of the family viewing the scapegoated child through this same distorted, negative lens.

For example, I once worked at a school for severely emotionally disturbed (SED) children. A five-year-old girl (who I will call Shannon) was sent to our school for "one last chance" before being ushered off to a supervised, locked unit. Shannon's (adoptive) parents were religious fundamentalists. Due to what they viewed as her uncontrollable, rebellious behavior, they agreed with their church minister that Shannon should be exorcised no less than three times over the course of a year. These exorcisms took place in front of their entire church congregation. Can you imagine Shannon's self-perception as a result of being told she was demonically possessed by both her church and her family, and what challenges she has faced to free herself from this dark and twisted narrative? I'd like to be able to tell you that this particular example of family scapegoating abuse is rare and extreme; sadly, I hear such stories from my clients and blog readers frequently.

The Scapegoat as "Mentally Ill" and "A Liar"

Many clients and readers of my blog have been described as mentally/emotionally ill and dishonest by one or more of their nuclear or extended family members. These people are invariably intelligent, well educated, and positively contributing to society. Many are quite successful in their personal and professional endeavors and are highly regarded within their communities. Not one of them has been diagnosed with psychosis or a severe Axis I disorder at any time in their life.

If these outrageous claims (which are actually a form of slander and a defamation of character) were not so egregious and personally/professionally harmful, they would be almost laughable. In any event, it certainly does seem to be the 'go-to' story in dysfunctional families that scapegoat one of their own.

While on the surface it may not seem to make much sense, this strangely common narrative that the scapegoated child/adult child is "mentally ill" is typical in families where aggressive, dominant family members seek to de-power and discredit the victim of their deliberately hostile behaviors. It's a defensive maneuver designed to establish the "sanity" of the abuser and the "insanity" of their victim. After all, who would believe the report of a "crazy" person?

"You're Faking It!"

My FSA research also revealed that children who are scapegoated may have their injuries and illnesses denied by a parent or primary caregiver, which causes them to invalidate their physical and 'felt-sense' experiences as adults. For example, stories I've collected via a survey I conducted include broken bones being ignored; severe infections (including sepsis) being minimized; and diseases being discounted and disbelieved by parents of the scapegoated child/adult child, despite the existence of medical reports that clearly confirmed their compromised condition (once they finally received medical attention).

This idea that the scapegoated family member dramatizes their injuries and "fakes" illnesses is frequently adopted by other nuclear and extended family members, which only serves to reinforce their deep sense of isolation and confusion. Because their physical experiences were invalidated, many FSA survivors report that as adults they deny their body's distress signals when they are not feeling well; minimize their injuries; and feel a sense of vague or acute shame when ill (as if they somehow shouldn't be, or it is a personal failing on their part that they are not well).

Many of my clients report that they dread going to the doctor for fear they will again have their injury or illness minimized or dismissed by someone in a position of authority, similar to when they were a child. While such neglect on a parent's part may seem incomprehensible on the surface (and is especially perplexing and disturbing to those whose parents were doctors, registered nurses, or otherwise employed in the field of healthcare), when viewed through the lens of *intergenerational transmissions* and the *family projection process* these failures to nurture and be responsive to their child's needs are better understood, as irrational as such negligence may seem.

The Devastating Impact of Family Scapegoating

Due to the harm done to the emerging self, the scapegoated child may struggle to identify wants and needs and will have difficulty forming secure attachments with important figures in their life. As an adult, the FSA survivor may lack the confidence to pursue goals and dreams and will have difficulty forming lasting, trusting attachments with others due to relational traumas sustained in childhood. They may feel that they don't have a right to be, to feel, or to express themselves authentically due to an inner sense of self-loathing rooted in toxic shame (I address 'toxic shame' and its negative effects in Chapter 13).

Many FSA survivors believe that something must be very wrong with them, but they are not sure what. They will often avoid talking about their negative family experiences with others due to a sense of shame or a fear of not being believed, which results in their becoming further isolated and increasingly vulnerable to depression. As a result of having the very core of who they are denied and redefined as children, the adult survivor of family scapegoating abuse will often find themselves feeling disconnected, dissociated, hopeless, and even passively and chronically suicidal as adults.

Scapegoated adult survivors have difficulty trusting others, and will struggle to form meaningful, secure attachments – including romantic and intimate ones. Because the 'scapegoat story' often follows them into adulthood and may continue after a parent's death via a dominant nuclear or extended family member, there may seem to be no way of remedying the situation other than to limit or end contact with some or all members of one's family-of-origin – a decision few in their life will support, much less understand.

Learn more about Murray Bowen's Family Systems Theory at www.thebowencenter.org

Next: *Take the* **Family Scapegoating Abuse (FSA) Assessment** *that I designed for my private practice clients based on my FSA research. You might want to record your 'Yes' responses so that you can review these when you're finished and perhaps reflect upon your experiences in a journal.*

2

FAMILY SCAPEGOATING ABUSE (FSA) SELF-TEST

The following describes a list of common conditions and symptoms associated with Family Scapegoating Abuse (FSA). As with *narcissistic abuse,* what I have named *family scapegoating abuse (FSA)* is a non–DSM (Diagnostic Statistical Manual of Mental Health Disorders) issue and the term is not formally used in clinical teaching or practice. As such, the questions included in this *FSA Self-Assessment* tool are based on my FSA research and clinical experience only.

This assessment is certainly not exhaustive and should not be used for diagnostic purposes. However, contemplating these questions may give you a sense of whether or not you may have been significantly impacted by being scapegoated in your family system. The more you answer "yes" to the questions, the more likely it is that you may be suffering from FSA.

Important Note: FSA survivors will often be diagnosed with one or more mental health conditions such as *Borderline* or

Histrionic Personality Disorder, Dissociative Identity Disorder, Generalized Anxiety Disorder; or *Major Depressive Disorder.* Rarely will the symptoms be recognized as **complex trauma (C-PTSD)** secondary to parental/familial maltreatment.

The World Health Organization (WHO) will be including C-PTSD as a billable and insurable diagnosis internationally in the next ICD-11 effective January 2022; however, C-PTSD is not yet recognized in the *Diagnostic Statistical Manual of Mental Disorder* (DSM) in the United States as a Mental Health diagnosis.

If you have been diagnosed with any of the above disorders (or similar) and you feel that your diagnosis does not accommodate some of your more acute symptoms — particularly if you were scapegoated persistently as a child — it may be useful for you to take this questionnaire with you when seeing a Mental Health professional so you can go over your experiences and answers together.

It may be that you will feel a sense of relief in recognizing that you are suffering from family scapegoating abuse (FSA) symptoms due to having your painful experiences validated, including specific types of traumatic events you may have endured for much of your life as the target of systemic scapegoating and abuse. The good news is that it is indeed possible to recover from family bullying, betrayal, and maltreatment, although some significant relational, behavioral, and life changes may need to be made in the process.

Please note that the terms 'primary caregivers' and 'parents' are used interchangeably throughout the questionnaire; however, siblings, in-laws, or other dominant nuclear and extended family members may also have participated in your scapegoating – Please adjust your answers accordingly.

Childhood Experiences

Do you believe that you were not well cared for and nurtured as a child within your family-of-origin?

Yes/No

Do you feel your primary caregivers neglected/abused you as a child?

Yes/No

Did you experience ongoing chronic stressors in your childhood (e.g., alcoholic family system, death, divorce, abandonment, neglect)?

Yes/No

Has a parent ever said something like, "I could have had a different/better life if it weren't for you," or implied you were an unhappy "accident"?

Yes/No

Did you have the sense that you wanted to escape from your family home, and had detailed fantasies of doing so?

Yes/No

Did you regularly daydream about being magically 'rescued' from your family home?

Yes/No

Were you 'gaslighted' growing up, e.g., were your everyday experiences and perceptions regularly denied or discounted by the power-holders in your family, such as your parents?

Yes/No

Did you feel that your parents treated you differently/worse than your siblings or others in your family?

Yes/No

Did you feel that your primary caregivers were insensitive to or denied and diminished your basic needs, including emotional?

Yes/No

Did you feel that you were essentially invisible to your parents, or did you wish to be invisible to avoid their negative attention?

Yes/No

REBECCA C. MANDEVILLE MFT

Did you lack any of the necessities of life (shelter, food, clothing, consistent nurturing)?

Yes/No

Did you regularly have the sense that one or both parents hated you?

Yes/No

Were you told by one or both parents that you were "bad" or was it implied that you were "different" or that something was wrong with you?

Yes/No

Did you feel that you were "bad", defective, or somehow not good enough as a child?

Yes/No

Did you feel like you had to constantly prove yourself to your parents to be worthy of love and positive regard?

Yes/No

Did your parent(s) point to one or more siblings as examples of what you needed to be and act like in order to 'deserve' or earn their love?

Yes/No

Did you grow up in your family home feeling like you were "walking on egg-shells" and needed to be careful not to upset anyone – one or both parents, especially?

Yes/No

Were you ever bullied outside the home, such as at school, an after-school group, summer camp, or in church?

Yes/No

Did one or both of your parents ever mention they were the scapegoat in their own family (e.g., they were seen by their parents or their grandparents as being a "bad" child?)

Yes/No

Did your caregiver(s) or any other close family members involved in your care (e.g., your grandparents) suffer from mental illness – whether treated or untreated?

Yes/No

Were you treated differently than your siblings growing up or now (i.e., less favorably)?

Yes/No

Did or do one or more siblings or cousins or other extended family members treat you poorly/speak negatively about you, either openly or covertly?

Yes/No

Did one or both parents tell relatives or friends that you were "crazy," "mentally ill," "emotionally unstable," or "a liar" when you challenged them on their poor treatment of you or as a means to discredit you to others to hide their own overt or covert abuse?

Yes/No

Did one or both parents promote a "story" about you to family or acquaintances and strangers whereby they are the "good", self-sacrificing parent and you were/are the "difficult" (perhaps ungrateful) child?

Yes/No

Present Circumstances

Do you feel that you are dissociated/not in your body?

Yes/No

Do you have difficulty with anger (either explosive anger or not being able to feel anger or both)?

Yes/No

Do you suffer from any one of the following: Anxiety, Depression, difficulty forming secure attachments?

Yes/No

Do you have a sense that you were betrayed by one or more family members (past or present)?

Yes/No

Do you ever contemplate suicide or have you attempted suicide?

Yes/No

Do you sometimes feel like you cannot trust your perception or sense of reality?

Yes/No

Do you struggle to find a sense of meaning and purpose in life?

Yes/No

Do you suffer from '*impostor syndrome*' at work/in your career (doubting your abilities and feeling like a fraud)?

Yes/No

Do you feel helpless, hopeless, or that you have lost all initiative?

Yes/No

Do you feel a chronic sense of shame, guilt, or self-blame?

Yes/No

Do you experience a sense of being maligned, cast out, different, 'othered', or otherwise stigmatized?

Yes/No

Do you feel that you are very different from other people and most could never understand you?

Yes/No

Are you preoccupied with your relationship with a caregiver(s) and nuclear/extended family members who neglected/abused/scapegoated you?

Yes/No

Do you sometimes feel that the caregiver(s) who neglected or abused you are all-powerful, despite the fact you are now an adult?

Yes/No

Do you feel strangely indebted to, or do you idealize, those in your family who neglected/abused/scapegoated you?

Yes/No

Are you convinced that you can one day "win" the love of nuclear/extended family who rejected/scapegoated you?

Yes/No

Do you find yourself quick to judge and perhaps scapegoat others?

Yes/No

Do you tend to isolate yourself socially or withdraw from others?

Yes/No

Do you have a difficult time finding or maintaining intimate relationships with others or feel insecure/anxious/mistrusting in any intimate relationship you are in?

Yes/No

Do you have a hope that one day your family will recognize you as a 'worthy' person, deserving of their care and love?

Yes/No

Have you had to limit or end contact with one or more family members to preserve/protect your own mental and emotional health?

Yes/No

Do you have a difficult time standing up for yourself or engaging in conflict?

Yes/No

Do you struggle with codependency/people-pleasing or addiction?

Yes/No

Do you have "revenge fantasies" toward any family members?

Yes/No

Do you suffer from symptoms of C-PTSD?

- Feelings of shame or guilt
- Difficulty controlling your emotions
- Periods of losing attention and concentration (dissociation)
- Physical symptom (headaches, dizziness, chest pains, stomach aches)
- Cutting yourself off from friends and family
- Relationship difficulties
- Destructive or risky behavior, such as self-harm, alcohol abuse, or drug abuse
- Suicidal thoughts

Yes/No

If you answered 'Yes' to <u>five or more</u> experiences listed in each category and the maltreatment toward you has been chronic/repetitive, you may be in the 'family scapegoat' role. As a consequence, you may be experiencing grave psycho-emotional distress and have trouble trusting others. You may feel isolated, angry, depressed, anxious, mistrusting, paranoid, frustrated, helpless, or hopeless.

You may also suffer from 'impostor syndrome', codependency, or addiction. You may feel 'triggered' or be experiencing negative emotions just from reading these FSA assessment questions, particularly if they hit close to home. If so, I suggest you take a few deep breaths and relax your body and your mind before continuing.

You may also want to journal some of your thoughts and feelings regarding aspects of this FSA assessment you most identified with and then share these reflections with your therapist or a trusted person in your life who feels emotionally safe and supportive.

Next: See if you identify with any of the following experiences common to scapegoated family members.

3

---

16 EXPERIENCES COMMON TO FSA SURVIVORS

"Am I the 'Family Scapegoat?'"

"How do I know if I'm in the 'family scapegoat' role?" I hear this question often from clients in my counseling and coaching practices. In addition to taking the FSA Self-Assessment in the previous chapter, reviewing the following sixteen experiences that are common to scapegoated children and adults can also be a way to determine if you are (or have been) in the 'family scapegoat' role:

1. You may identify as being 'codependent' or 'highly sensitive' and 'empathic'. You may 'fawn' (people-please) to avoid conflict. Alternatively, you may have no problem setting boundaries and will defend yourself without hesitation if you feel you are being disrespected or violated in some manner.

2. You may have difficulty expressing your feelings because at a very young age you learned to be careful about revealing too much of yourself as it would be used against you by family members. You may have been told by a parent or other family member that you are "cold," "unloving," "insensitive," "too sensitive," "heartless," "selfish," or "dramatic" by a scapegoating parent when you did attempt to express your honest emotions and experiences, including when you were very young. As a result of stuffing down (repressing) your feelings and natural responses, you may experience various physical ailments or struggle with addiction, codependency, anxiety, depression, or obsessive-compulsive behaviors.

3. You are made to feel solely responsible for the quality of your relationship with a parent, primary caregiver, dominant sibling, or others in your family; if there are 'problems' in the relationship, it is viewed as being your fault, no matter what.

4. You have been labeled "a liar," "crazy," or "mentally/ emotionally ill" by one or more family members. You may have distanced yourself from select relatives as a result of continued character assassination in an attempt to protect yourself and minimize personal harm.

5. One or more family members have been physically, sexually, emotionally, or mentally abusive toward you (including 'gaslighting' you, i.e., denying, distorting, and twisting events to show themselves in a better light at your expense).

6. Nuclear or extended family members and/or non-family members were informed by a parent/primary caregiver that you were a troubled, 'problem' child and were difficult to deal with and not to be trusted or believed.

7. If you try to inform others within or outside the family of the abuse you are experiencing (as a child, or years later as an adult), you are not believed and the abusive family member will deny their behavior (often via a 'smear campaign' whereby you are once again "a liar" or somehow mentally/emotionally defective).

8. Your parent(s) may have objectified and dehumanized you in various ways, e.g., you were told you were "difficult" or were made to feel incompetent and not 'good enough'. You may have

been maligned by a parent to others, including in your presence (e.g., "Janie was such a difficult baby, she has so many emotional problems") – including to friends or dates you brought home.

9. You may be accused of 'faking' a genuine illness by one or more people in your family (nuclear or extended).

10. You blame yourself for any relationship difficulties you experience as an adult, fearing that there is something innately wrong with you and that you are somehow damaged and defective.

11. You feel uncomfortable around your family-of-origin (separate, different, 'not part of'); you feel trapped in a role of some kind, feel stifled and constricted in your interactions (e.g., a sense of having to 'walk on eggshells') and are not able to relax and feel like your 'true self' around your family. This feeling of 'dis-ease' might translate into other areas of your life, resulting in your feeling like an 'outsider'. This might in turn cause you to behave in ways that contribute to your sense of social isolation due to being unable to trust others or take interpersonal risks.

12. You may have difficulty forming healthy attachments and trusting, loving connections and you may blame yourself for this. You may be attracted to addicts, narcissists, or abusers, know it's unhealthy, but

continue to make self-damaging relationship choices.

13. You have struggled with *anxiety, depression,* or '*imposter syndrome,* and may have been diagnosed with a Mental Health disorder.

14. You are 'the client that cannot be helped', i.e., you have consulted with various Mental Health professionals but no clinician or counselor can help you figure out why you feel the way you do or get to the heart of the matter so that you can heal at a deep, core level. Talk therapy, mindfulness-based practices, or medications help a little, but not much (unless the healing professional understands you are an adult survivor of child abuse).

15. Your family minimizes or ignores your personal or professional accomplishments. No matter how highly regarded you may be outside of your family-of-origin, to your family you are essentially a "fake" and have somehow managed to fool everyone by pretending you are something that you couldn't possibly be (e.g., successful, healthy, high functioning, respected in your profession, etc.). This may contribute to your experience of 'imposter syndrome'.

16. You may have had no choice but to reduce or limit contact with one or more family members to protect your own mental and emotional health. You may

question yourself for this decision or feel guilty, 'bad',
or 'wrong' for distancing yourself from your family.
Nuclear or extended family members may openly
state to others that you deserve to be an outcast and
take no responsibility for their part in the
dysfunctional interactions, particularly if their actions
toward you were overtly or covertly abusive.

If you strongly identify with any of the above experiences,
you may be in the 'scapegoat' role in your family. As in the
last chapter, you may want to journal some of your thoughts
and feelings regarding what aspects of the above family
scapegoating experiences you relate to and share these
awarenesses with your therapist or a trusted person in your life
whom you feel emotionally safe sharing your insights with.

---

*In the next section, I'll discuss the scapegoated adult's experience of
disenfranchised grief as related to the various losses associated with
family scapegoating abuse.*

4

FSA SURVIVORS AND DISENFRANCHISED GRIEF

Family scapegoating abuse survivors often experience 'disenfranchised grief' – an apt term coined by grief researcher Ken Doka. Per Doka (1989), disenfranchised grief is experienced when someone suffers a loss that is not (or cannot) be openly acknowledged, socially sanctioned, or publicly mourned.

Double Binds and Unrecognized Grief

I have yet to work with a client suffering from family scapegoating abuse who was not experiencing a myriad of emotions related to their painful family experiences, including confusion, frustration, anger, sadness, hopelessness, and despair.

However, rarely will a client impacted by family scapegoating dynamics view themselves as someone who may be grieving due to the many losses associated with being in the 'scapegoat' role. They are typically somewhat numb and dissociated from their feelings, or they are filled with a sense of intense anger and rage regarding how members of their family have treated them.

Before initiating services with me, they may have been finding support in forums that focus on healing from *narcissistic abuse,* which can serve as a 'safe space' for the expression of rage toward their "narc" (narcissistic) parent(s). However, conversations about *loss and grief* in regard to being scapegoated are less evident in forums my clients have participated in.

Anger, of course, is an expected and understandable emotion when one has experienced grave injustices, whether individual or systemic. Caring about justice and feeling injustices have been done, or caring about and loving family that has put you in a position whereby you can't engage with them as it is detrimental to your mental and emotional well-being, can indeed be angering.

However, because anger is such a powerful emotion, it is easy to get stuck in it, especially when no clear pathway to resolving or ending the parental or family maltreatment is evident. This can result in the sense of being caught in a double-bind, i.e., the scapegoated adult suffers if they remain engaged with their family, and they suffer if they end contact with those they may still love. However, if and when the FSA sufferer finally has their anger, pain, and sense of injustice heard and acknowledged, they will likely find themselves diving deep into their grief.

Based on my years of experience working with clients in my psychotherapy and coaching practices, the FSA survivor's experience of disenfranchised grief is associated with (but not limited to) the following circumstances:

1. Lost family connections: Specifically, the FSA survivor's grief regarding having limited or ended family contact is not recognized by others. This is particularly true in cases where the FSA survivor has chosen to limit or go 'no contact' with abusive family members to protect their own mental and emotional health.

2. Lost community and social connections: Many FSA survivors feel they have no choice but to relocate so as not to be forever stigmatized in their community due to family 'smear

campaigns' designed to malign the FSA survivor's reputation and character.

3. Not being recognized as a griever – and being viewed as the cause of their grief: The FSA survivor may be blamed or judged by others for distancing themselves from abusive family members (e.g., "Did you really have to end contact? I'm sure your family loves you and would want to see you, there's no reason for you to feel so alone, why don't you reach out to them?"), and therefore not deserving of support or even the right to grieve.

4. Grief is masked by intense feelings of anger, betrayal, and hurt: FSA survivors have been harmed and maltreated by the very people who were supposed to love and care for them the most. The scapegoating parent, sibling, cousin, in-law, or grandparent will typically not ever acknowledge their harmful or abusive acts, much less apologize for them. It is therefore understandable why many scapegoated adults feel a chronic sense of 'righteous anger' – even rage – regarding how they have been treated. The fact that they may also be grieving specific losses related to being scapegoated and their recovery process (e.g., ending contact with abusive family members and no longer being able to see siblings, nieces, nephews, and other relatives) typically goes unrecognized.

5. Feeling isolated in their FSA experiences: As family scapegoating abuse can be subtle and insidious, many FSA survivors have difficulty identifying and discussing what has

happened to them in their families (especially if they are also suffering from complex trauma symptoms (C-PTSD). Sadly, it is common for the FSA survivor's stories of maltreatment or extreme abuse at the hands of a parent or other family member to be dismissed and discounted, including by those they may have most counted on for help, support, and validation. And because FSA survivors, like other abuse survivors, often experience unconscious 'toxic shame', they may feel faulty, defective, and undeserving of love, respect, comfort, and consideration, which further isolates them and deprives them of meaningful support.

Recognizing Grief as FSA Survivors

Many people are familiar with Kubler-Ross's <u>Five Stages of Grief</u>, which are *Denial; Anger; Bargaining; Depression; Acceptance.*

This model for understanding how we heal from devastating losses (a model that was originally created to address losses related to death and dying) has been challenged over the years for a variety of reasons, including the implication that the grief process is linear.

I agree that these stages are not linear – we may move in and out of any of these states at any time. However, when assessing a new FSA recovery client, I can sense during the first session whether or not they have consciously grieved the various losses associated with being scapegoated by one's family.

If my client is obsessively preoccupied with specific people, situations, and past (possibly traumatic) events, it can be a critical aspect of their recovery process to explore underlying feelings of grief and loss due to being the family 'identified patient'. It is also important to recognize that because many FSA survivors are simultaneously suffering from symptoms of complex trauma, the process of grieving and accepting what has happened to them in their family can become particularly complicated, and will usually require their working intensively with a *trauma-informed counselor or coach* who has expertise in the area of family systems, complicated grief, and recovering from *adverse childhood experiences* (ACE) and family abuse .

Many of my FSA recovery clients initially present as being in the stages of *denial* and *bargaining*. Even in the most severe cases of scapegoating, they at times simply can't believe that the maltreatment they have experienced within their family qualifies as mental and emotional abuse. Some clients are well beyond the denial stage and can easily access their justifiable sense of anger and will be drawn to self-help books, online forums, and social media groups that allow them to identify and share their understandable outrage and pain.

While each person's recovery journey is unique, I have found both personally and as a clinician that if grief and the idea of grieving are avoided, deep and lasting healing from the trauma of family scapegoating abuse can be difficult to achieve. Doka's concept of '*disenfranchised grief*' has therefore been a gift to many of my counseling and coaching clients, for within his descriptions of isolation and loss, they often find a critical aspect of their own grief process reflected.

Note: For an insightful commentary on the grieving process, visit David Kessler's website (www.grief.com) – He co-authored books on grief and grieving with Kubler-Ross and addresses misunderstandings commonly associated with her original model (which, as Kessler emphasizes, has evolved over time).

———

Another serious consequence of family scapegoating abuse often goes unrecognized, misdiagnosed, or undiagnosed: In the next two chapters, we will look at the relationship between FSA and complex trauma (C-PTSD).

5

FSA AND COMPLEX TRAUMA (C-PTSD)

Adult survivors of family scapegoating abuse (FSA) *have historically been diagnosed with one or more mental health conditions that ignore the trauma symptoms they are regularly experiencing. Rarely will their most distressing symptoms be recognized as Complex post-traumatic stress disorder (C-PTSD) secondary to growing up in an unstable, non-nurturing, dangerous, rejecting, or abusive family environment.*

Adult Survivors of FSA and Complex Trauma

Many adult survivors of dysfunctional family systems and childhood abuse suffer from anxiety, panic attacks, and anger management issues. They may have been diagnosed in the past with *Generalized Anxiety Disorder*, *Major Depressive Disorder*, or *Dissociative Identity Disorder (DID)*.

In addition to the above disorders, several adult survivors of FSA have shared with me during the psychotherapy intake process that they have been diagnosed in the past with *Attention Deficit Hyperactive Disorder (ADHD)*, *Bipolar Disorder*, *Obsessive-Compulsive Disorder (OCD)*, and *Agoraphobia*. Others have been diagnosed as having a personality disorder (*Borderline Personality Disorder*, especially) or an attachment disorder. They will also often present with *codependency* or *addiction* and may be in an unfulfilling or abusive relationship.

As related to my clinical work with adult survivors seeking to recover from FSA, it is my experience that the non-nurturing, toxic, and covertly or openly abusive family environments my clients grew up in (and had no means of escaping from) have contributed to their experiencing symptoms of *Complex post-traumatic stress disorder (C-PTSD)*, which is also referred to as Complex Trauma disorder) secondary to psycho-emotional (and at times physical/sexual) abuse.

Complex PTSD Versus PTSD

Most of my clients have never heard of C-PTSD and are not aware of how it might apply to them, although many have heard of PTSD. I will therefore explain that complex PTSD differs from PTSD in that the trauma sufferer has been exposed to **repeated and prolonged traumatic events** which, in many cases, may apply to a dysfunctional, abusive, or otherwise traumatizing family environment.

Regrettably, complex PTSD is still not recognized in the *Diagnostic Statistical Manual of Mental Disorders* (DSM) in the United States as a diagnosis. Because Complex post-traumatic stress disorder is closely related to Post-traumatic stress disorder, some savvy clinicians will acknowledge a C-PTSD diagnosis via specific PTSD coding currently offered in the DSM. Others may diagnose anxiety or depression while psycho-educating their client on the features of C-PTSD as part of formulating an efficacious treatment plan.

Symptoms of Complex PTSD

As the *National Center for PTSD* website notes, Dr. Judith Herman of Harvard University proposed in 1988 that a new diagnosis, *complex PTSD*, was needed to describe the symptoms of long-term trauma. Per Dr. Miller, such symptoms (which are now acknowledged by the *U.S. Department of Veterans Affairs*) include:

- Behavioral difficulties (e.g. impulsivity, aggressiveness, sexual acting out, alcohol/drug misuse and self-destructive behavior)

- Emotional difficulties (e.g. affect lability, rage, depression, and panic)

- Cognitive difficulties (e.g. dissociation and pathological changes in personal identity)

- Interpersonal difficulties (e.g. chaotic personal relationships)

- Somatization (resulting in many visits to medical practitioners)

As per the *National Health Service (NHS)* in the United Kingdom (which also now includes a page on C-PTSD on their website), complex PTSD may be diagnosed in adults or children who have repeatedly experienced traumatic events, such as violence, neglect, or abuse. The symptoms of complex PTSD are listed on the NHS website as:

- Feelings of shame or guilt

- Difficulty controlling your emotions

- Periods of losing attention and concentration (dissociation)

- Physical symptom (headaches, dizziness, chest pains, stomach aches)

- Cutting yourself off from friends and family

- Relationship difficulties

- Destructive or risky behavior, such as self-harm, alcohol abuse, or drug abuse

- Suicidal thoughts

Family Scapegoating Abuse (FSA) Symptoms

Based on my research on what I named *family scapegoating abuse* (a non-DSM issue), as well as over 20 years of clinical experience working with adult survivors, adult survivors of family scapegoating typically experience several of the following symptoms and issues, some which are also suggestive of complex trauma (C-PTSD):

- Intense feelings of guilt or shame

- Intense feelings of anger or rage

- Intense feelings of sadness and disenfranchised grief

- Intense feelings of desperation and despair

- "Stuffing" or deliberately withholding feelings/emotions

- Dissociation

- Traumatic nightmares (rooted in the memory of the event; the traumatic event is re-experienced)

- Intrusive thoughts/sensations/emotions/flashbacks

- Flight, Fight, Freeze, or Fawn response to perceived conflicts/threats

- Physical symptoms, such as headaches, racing heart or heart palpitations, sweating, dizziness, chest pains, hives, and stomach aches

- Family disconnection (by necessity or by choice)

- Self-destructive behavior

- Low Self-Esteem/Self-Hatred (feeling 'bad', 'wrong', defective, damaged, worthless)

- Learned helplessness

- Relationship difficulties or a sense of feeling disconnected from others

- Fear of intimacy

- Inability to trust others for fear of being betrayed/abandoned/hurt

- Persistent abandonment fears (at times includes *abandonment depression*)

- Codependency (this can include high sensitivity to people's emotional states and being over-focused on others)

- Inability to negotiate interpersonal boundaries

- Addiction/Alcoholism

- Loss of control of emotions/anger outbursts

- Flashbacks

- Ruminating (reliving harmful interpersonal events

experienced with scapegoating family members)

- Paranoia

- Anxiety

- Panic Attacks

- Depression

- Suicidal thoughts

Most clients being treated in my practice who report mental and emotional distress secondary to family scapegoating issues have at least **five** of the above FSA or C-PTSD symptoms. **It is my clinical opinion that FSA symptoms that overlap with C-PTSD symptoms always warrant further investigation.** This is because identifying C-PTSD symptoms early on in the therapy process will help the clinician to build a more robust, trauma-informed treatment plan, which has the potential to greatly benefit the client.

C-PTSD as a Distinct Diagnosis

Due to C-PTSD not being formally recognized as a diagnosis in most countries, resources for those that suffer from symptoms of complex trauma are limited, including access to appropriately trained Mental Health professionals. However, the World Health Organization (WHO) will be including C-PTSD as a *billable and insurable* diagnosis internationally in the next ICD (11) effective January 2022, which will put pressure on the American Psychological Association (APA) in the United States to recognize it as a legitimate diagnosis.

As of 2013, Post-traumatic stress disorder is included in a new category in the current DSM (5): *Trauma and Stressor-Related Disorders*. It is this category that lends itself most to trauma caused by repeated and prolonged (over months or years) stressors, but in my opinion this method of diagnosing fails to adequately acknowledge the primary symptoms associated with C-PTSD, which can be frustrating to trauma-informed clinicians when diagnosing their clients or patients.

Complex PTSD (which is sometimes interchanged with terms such as *complex relational trauma, developmental trauma,* and *interpersonal trauma)* is a relatively recent concept. With the recognition of complex PTSD (C-PTSD) by the *World Health Organization* (WHO), healthcare providers around the world are slowly gaining access to critical information about complex/chronic forms of trauma experienced by children and adults, including adult survivors of childhood abuse and neglect.

Although the *American Psychiatric Association* does not acknowledge C-PTSD in the current DSM (5), clinicians practicing in the United States may now point to the WHO's recognition of C-PTSD as a legitimate diagnosis when inviting their clients to explore the possibility that they may have been 'under'-diagnosed (or outright misdiagnosed) in the past. This is especially important because when trauma symptoms go unacknowledged and unaddressed, treatment of the client and their symptoms is much less likely to be effective.

The International Trauma Questionnaire (ITQ)

Numerous studies are currently taking place around the world as part of the standardization process of the *International Trauma Questionnaire (ITQ)* used to assess the core features of both C-PTSD and PTSD.

The ITQ has been used, or is currently in use, in 29 countries across six continents. Preliminary evidence suggests that the ITQ is an instrument that produces reliable and valid scores and can adequately distinguish between PTSD and C-PTSD cross-culturally.

Interestingly, in the United States, studies using the ITQ indicated that women were more than twice as likely to meet criteria for both PTSD and C-PTSD than men. Given that the most frequently endorsed DSO (disturbance of self organization) cluster was negative self-concept, the critical role problems in negative self-concept may play in C-PTSD would seem to warrant special attention for clinicians working with female clients who report being chronically scapegoated, blamed, shamed, neglected, or rejected by a parent or other significant family member.

Next, I'll present a case study illustrating the overlapping symptoms of FSA and C-PTSD.

6

LILY: A CASE STUDY

Complex trauma (C-PTSD) describes exposure to multiple traumatic events and the long-term impact of this exposure. It is therefore not surprising that children who were the target of family scapegoating abuse (FSA) are often suffering from undiagnosed and untreated complex trauma today.

Complex Trauma and the Scapegoated Adult Child

As illustrated in the previous chapter, FSA and C-PTSD are closely related. Whereas simple trauma refers to one single event which is obvious and definable, such as an accident or bodily assault, complex trauma describes exposure to multiple traumatic events and the long-term impact of this exposure. It is therefore not surprising that children who were chronically scapegoated by their parents or other significant family members may be suffering from undiagnosed and untreated complex trauma as adults.

Because family scapegoating abuse doesn't magically stop when the child matures into an adult, the scapegoating will most likely continue, resulting in the adult child being 'triggered' and re-traumatized from repeated exposures to family members who continue to maltreat them, whether openly or covertly.

Scapegoated adults who believed that the chronic maltreatment would end with the death of a parent may be shocked to discover that the abuse continues on via a dominant family member (such as a sibling), who adopts the false narrative promoted by the deceased parent that the FSA target is defective, "crazy," a "liar," a "faker," or otherwise fundamentally "bad".

Lily: A Client Case Study

The following case study serves as an example of how family scapegoating abuse (FSA) symptoms may sometimes overlap with complex trauma (C–PTSD) symptoms:

When Lily initiated psychotherapy services with me, she reported feeling "anxious, lonely, hopeless, and lost." She experienced deep fears of being rejected and avoided dating as a result. She had difficulty trusting others and struggled to set boundaries, which she felt was negatively impacting her relationships with others, including with her team at work.

Lily was especially worried because she was feeling increasingly distant from others and "numb and disconnected." Lily also shared she often had "bad dreams" in which she was taken hostage or was suddenly being shot at with no means of escaping or getting help. She also experienced occasional panic attacks when visiting her parents and avoided seeing them as a result, and she felt guilt, embarrassment, and shame around this apparent loss of physiological and emotional control.

During our intake session, I learned that Lily grew up with the knowledge that her father had been disappointed with her because she wasn't born a boy. When he verbally attacked her as a child by calling her "stupid," "ugly," and "fat" (such incidents were frequent), she figured it was because he was upset she "wasn't a boy but some part of me knew I didn't deserve it, even when I was very young." Her father also drank too much at times and would become hostile and irrational, screaming at both her and her mother for various imagined offenses until he passed out.

Because she was an only child, Lily felt the weight of her father's disappointment more acutely as she got older. Her father's active psycho-emotional and verbal abuse toward her gradually turned into disinterest and neglect by the time she entered adolescence. She did feel somewhat supported and loved by her mother, but couldn't help but believe that her mother must be disappointed in her as well, given she couldn't have any more children and her father had so desperately wanted a son to "carry on the family name."

Psycho -Education and Assessing Overlapping Symptoms

After reviewing Lily's presenting issues and symptoms during the intake process, I explained to her that her father's chronic emotional neglect and "blaming and shaming" behaviors (including his disparaging comments about her appearance) – and his disinterest in her as she got older – were in fact forms of cover and overt psycho-emotional abuse. This initially surprised her but also gave her a sense of relief. "I thought there was something wrong with me that I just couldn't get over my childhood – I never realized that what I went through was abusive. I thought abuse was mostly physical. Somehow having a name for what happened to me makes me feel better."

Later, I let Lily know that it might be wise to assess her for symptoms of complex trauma (C-PTSD) concerning her having been mentally and emotionally abused as a child. Lily expressed confusion, replying that she thought "PTSD was only for people who fought in wars and things like that."

Lily's response was understandable and also typical of clients that have never heard of C-PTSD and are not aware of how it might apply to them. I explained to Lily that complex PTSD differs from PTSD in that it acknowledges repeated and prolonged traumatic events experienced in childhood from which there is no escape, which is often applicable to the scapegoated child's experience of their dysfunctional, rejecting family environment.

In Lily's case, learning that what she experienced in childhood constituted abuse and having her symptoms of complex trauma identified, assessed, and validated allowed her to view herself and her mental health challenges with compassion. At the same time, understanding that she was an adult survivor of child abuse and had symptoms of C-PTSD instilled her with a sense of hope that recovery was possible. This in turn allowed her to commit to an efficacious trauma-informed treatment pathway designed to address both family scapegoating abuse (past and present) and her symptoms of complex trauma.

Next, I'll explore scapegoating as related to **Betrayal Trauma Theory (BTT)**.

7

SCAPEGOATING AS FAMILY BETRAYAL

Betrayal trauma theory (BTT) is defined as a trauma perpetrated by someone with whom the victim is close to and reliant upon for support and survival. BTT addresses situations in which people or institutions that a person relies upon for protection, resources, and survival violate the trust or well-being of that person (Freyd, 2008). Next, we'll look at how betrayal trauma and family scapegoating abuse interrelate.

What Is Betrayal Trauma Theory?

Betrayal Trauma Theory (BTT) was first introduced by Dr. Jennifer J. Freyd in 1994. BTT is a concept I share early on when working with clients suffering from family scapegoating abuse (FSA). BTT is relevant to discussions of FSA in that it is rooted in the recognition of the *dissociation* a child might experience in response to living in an unsafe, unpredictable, or hostile environment. The child 'forgets' the abuse, i.e. they do not consciously remember it. It should be noted that dissociation closely correlates with the 'freeze state' which instinctively occurs in response to traumatic events and environments (the other states being fight/flight/fawn).

BTT asserts that betrayal acts as the precursor to dissociation, meaning, the dissociation occurs as a means of preserving the relationship with the primary caregiver or other important family figures the child feels dependent upon for their survival. Because a child must rely on their caregiver for support and safety, they are more likely to dissociate ('split off') traumatic experiences from conscious awareness when experiencing betrayals of trust.

Child abuse inherently includes betrayal trauma because those that the child most depended on to care for and protect them (e.g., parents, teachers, relatives, etc.) instead actively harmed them and broke their trust. It is also important to note that the child does not need to be consciously aware of the caregiver's betrayal to experience BTT. According to DePrince and Freyd (2002a):

> "The role of betrayal in betrayal trauma theory was initially considered an implicit but central aspect of some situations. If a child is being mistreated by a caregiver he or she is dependent upon, this is by definition betrayal, whether the child recognizes the betrayal explicitly or not. Indeed, the memory impairment and gaps in awareness that betrayal trauma theory predicted were assumed to serve in part to ward off conscious awareness of mistreatment to promote the dependent child's survival goals ... While conscious appraisals of betrayal may be inhibited at the time of trauma and for as long as the trauma victim is dependent upon the perpetrator, eventually the trauma survivor may become conscious of strong feelings of betrayal" (page 74-75).

The Lasting Negative Effects of Betrayal Trauma and FSA

Although betrayal trauma does not meet the diagnostic criteria for PTSD, I propose that, like FSA, it is clinically appropriate to consider betrayal trauma as contributing to the manifestation of complex trauma symptoms (C-PTSD), given that BTT develops in response to relational trauma and chronic environmental stressors.

Specifically: When the family environment feels unsafe, threatening, or hostile, and there is no means of escape due to age and various types of dependency, the child is vulnerable to developing signs and symptoms of complex trauma, which will often intensify when they are adults.

For the scapegoated child in a dysfunctional family, the intrapsychic dilemma is particularly acute: Instead of feeling loved, supported, accepted, valued, and cared about, they are often actively and openly rejected, shamed, blamed, and betrayed by their parent(s) or significant 'others' when they are aggressively or covertly attacked by those they most rely on to survive.

The scapegoated child is also likely to experience overwhelming levels of 'toxic shame' (to be discussed in Chapter 13), resulting in their experiencing themselves as fundamentally "bad," "wrong," "less than," and "defective" at a subconscious level. The resulting psycho-emotional distress can be acute and follow them life-long, negatively impacting their relationships with others as adults.

Challenging the Family Homeostasis

It can also be the case that as the scapegoated child becomes older, they will openly reject the family narrative that portrays them as being perennially in the wrong, 'bad', defective, or the only one at fault when there is interpersonal conflict within their family system (this may include their spouse/partner's family system as well). They will likely experience increased relational distress (and possibly trauma) as a direct consequence of challenging the dysfunctional *family projection process* and general *family homeostasis,* or balance, that requires them to remain in the 'scapegoat' role.

With no means of effectively addressing the situation due to being chronically disempowered by the (family) system they find themselves within, the FSA survivor will often become distraught and hopeless. They might turn to a sibling or other relative they view as an "ally" for help and support, only to be told, "I'm sorry, but I just don't want to get involved." To the victim of family scapegoating, this can feel like a form of relational abandonment and betrayal as well.

As they enter adulthood, the FSA survivor will likely struggle to form stable, intimate relationships due to past experiences of having their trust betrayed. Alternatively, they may find themselves in abusive relationships as an adult, unconsciously recreating their childhood experiences of interpersonal harm and betrayal.

In the next chapter, I discuss scapegoating abuse as it relates to intergenerational trauma and the family 'empath' or 'truth-teller', who (based on my FSA research) often finds themselves in the 'scapegoat' role.

8

INTERGENERATIONAL TRAUMA AND THE FAMILY EMPATH

As painful as it is to be scapegoated by your family, you might be surprised to learn that there are positive, empowering aspects associated with the 'scapegoat' role, as described in the original biblical story of the 'scapegoat ritual of atonement.' It may be that certain qualities you possess, such as intuition, empathy, and compassion, led to your becoming the target of family scapegoating abuse, as paradoxical and confusing as this may initially seem.

The Story of the Scapegoat Ritual

The term *'scapegoat'* originated from a story in the Old Testament (Leviticus 16: 1-34). In this ancient tale that is associated with the ceremonies of the *Day of Atonement*, Aaron had to choose a goat to take on the sins of the tribe, i.e., the collective). This goat was then cast out into the desert.

A weak, domesticated goat would have likely died a short time after being left to fend for itself. Therefore, the goat Aaron selected had to be very strong and robust so it could fulfill its purpose of relieving the tribe of its 'sins', which is why Aaron had likely chosen it most carefully. Meaning, it was imperative that this goat survive after being cast out from its herd.

I am keenly aware that if you are reading this introductory guide on family scapegoating abuse you may be in a great amount of emotional pain. You may feel vulnerable, raw, and weak as a result of being deprived of the protection of your own family (or 'tribe'). It is therefore very important that I emphasize that the scapegoat in this story was the most robust, strongest goat in the herd. *That is why it was chosen.*

It has been my observation that the 'scapegoat child' is often the most psychologically-minded, emotionally sensitive, intuitive, and 'aware' person in their family. Because they are so energetically sensitive, empathic, and open, they, like Aaron's sacrificial goat, may become the unconscious bearer of the family's 'sins'.

Based on my FSA research I'd like to go one step further by proposing that it is not only the burden of the family's collective 'sin' or 'shadow' (i.e., the disowned, unconscious intrapsychic aspects associated with the *nuclear family emotional process* that the FSA sufferer carries for the family), **but the heavy weight of unacknowledged** *intergenerational trauma* **(also referred to as** *multigenerational* **or** *transgenerational trauma).*

The Unconscious Effects of Intergenerational Trauma

As discussed previously in this guide, in *Family Systems* theory the 'scapegoat' is associated with the clinical term '*identified patient*'. The scapegoating of a child or adult child is most often (but not always) the result of an unconscious *family projection process* that supports maladaptive emotional and behavioral coping patterns that are 'transmitted' between generations.

Given this, I hypothesize that the 'scapegoat' is in actuality the repository of <u>intergenerational trauma,</u> **versus the more literal family 'sins'.** Remember, the selection of the scapegoated family member is fueled by unconscious processes. It's not like the family holds a meeting and says, "We're going to choose Janie (or Johnny) to be our family scapegoat so we can project our collective shadow onto them and feel better about ourselves!" The projection process that supports the 'othering' of one's own flesh and blood is far more subtle and insidious than that.

In dysfunctional family systems, imprisoning 'roles' are (unconsciously) assigned and 'inherited'. This is why in many (if not most) dysfunctional families you will find that there is a 'scapegoat' (aka 'problem child') in every generation. As mentioned, this role is not static and may be projected onto various family members over a given period of time.

As the family 'identified patient', the scapegoated child acts as a 'container' for the family's unfelt, repressed anxiety and trauma. Other roles common to dysfunctional families are the 'golden child' (who is idealized and can do no wrong), along with the 'clown', the 'hero', and the 'rescuer/caretaker'. (Read more about the latest epigenetics studies that suggest we may in fact 'inherit' trauma in the online article, *Can the Legacy of Trauma Be Passed Down the Generations?*).

There's often no rhyme or reason as to why a particular child becomes the 'scapegoat' in a 'toxic' and distressed family system. In some cases the child may have a highly traumatized or personality-disordered parent and is scapegoated due to the parent projecting onto their child their own disowned (shadowy, unconscious) parts (e.g., the parts of themselves they find unacceptable or contrary to who they believe themselves to be).

For example, one of my clients had a grandfather who had

been made to feel very ashamed of being Native American by religious missionaries as a boy, and so he never discussed his heritage. He married an Irish woman and the family identified primarily as 'Irish-American'. However, my client looked strongly Native American. Although it cannot be known for sure, he feels it is likely that this was one of the reasons his grandfather was unspeakably cruel toward him until the day he died.

I've had other clients and *FSA Survey* respondents share that they had a very controlling, dominating, narcissistic-type parent who scapegoated them for not 'obeying' them and behaving in a submissive way.

I've also seen many cases where a parent makes one child "good" (aka 'the golden child') and the other (scapegoated) child "bad". This is common in parents who have a personality disorder and engage in an unconscious process called *splitting*, such as parents with *Borderline Personality Disorder* (as discussed earlier in this guide).

Interestingly, a high percentage of *FSA Survey* respondents identified as being the '*truth-teller*' or '*Empath*' in their family (I discuss the Empath and scapegoating in more detail in the next section).

Suffice it to say that these unconscious family projection processes that dehumanize and objectify children by imprisoning them in one-dimensional roles result in the continuation of dysfunctional patterns of behavior that are passed on from one generation to the next like a poisonous family recipe.

The Empath and Scapegoating

Empaths are highly sensitive individuals who feel and 'take in' the emotions of the people around them and may develop physical symptoms because of their acute sensitivities. Whether the empath has these abilities due to 'nature' or 'nurture' is still up for debate, but as an empath myself, I would say it is a combination of both.

There may now be scientific evidence supporting the empath's experience as well: Researchers have discovered a specialized group of brain cells that are responsible for the experience of compassion. These cells enable one to mirror emotions, to share another person's pain, to feel their fear or their joy. Given this, empaths may have *hyper-responsive mirror neurons* which allows them to resonate deeply and profoundly with other people's feelings.

The empath has greater access to their 'felt-sense' experiences of events, people, places, and things and tends to be highly intuitive and aware of the emotions and energies of those around them. At times, they may struggle to intellectualize and express their direct knowledge from their intuitive senses and feelings, causing them to withdraw or perhaps 'act out'.

Those who identify more as being a *highly sensitive person (HSP)* also qualify as empaths in that they tend to feel the emotions of others just as empaths do. At the same time, being an HSP also involves being more sensitive to all sensory input, not just emotions, which might feel overwhelming at times to some.

My FSA research suggests that it is typically the most empathic, intuitive member of the family who is cast in the 'scapegoat' role, regardless of their sibling position (i.e., oldest, middle, youngest) or their age.

I suspect that the reason for this is that empath-types tend to be 'truth-seers', 'truth-seekers', and (sometimes) the 'truth-tellers' in their family, making them more likely to speak out when they see or experience injustices or abuse. Being sensitive to others' pain, they may also defend or protect siblings or a parent, making them vulnerable to attacks from aggressive family members. **As such, the empath may be viewed as a threat by the dysfunctional power-holder(s) in their family** (typically a primary caregiver, but not always), who must then de-power the empath to maintain control of the family narrative that serves them, a narrative that leaves them blameless for any dysfunction or abuse in the family.

Empaths and HSP-types who loathe conflict typically develop the trauma response of 'fawning' in response to family scapegoating abuse. This maladaptive survival (or coping) response is also referred to as 'appeasing', 'people-pleasing', or 'codependency'. I'll be discussing 'fawning' and 'maladaptive survival responses' in the next chapter.

9

THE TRAUMA RESPONSE OF 'FAWNING'

If you identify as being highly sensitive, intuitive, or an 'empath', you may tend to avoid conflict as much as possible and will deny your truth in an attempt to make those you feel dependent upon or care about comfortable. Although you might easily stand up for others, you may find it difficult or impossible to stand up for yourself when being maltreated by others – including in regard to your family. You may instead seek to 'appease' those who treat you badly as a means of avoiding conflict, or deny the sad truth of your situation altogether. But in reality, 'fawning' and maladaptive coping behaviors serve no one in the end.

Fawning as Maladaptive Survival Response

The 'fawn' response is an instinctual response associated with a need to avoid conflict and trauma via appeasing behaviors. For children, fawning behaviors can be a *maladaptive survival or coping response* which developed as a means of coping with a non-nurturing or abusive parent. MFT and complex trauma (C-PTSD) expert *Pete Walker* coined the term 'fawn' response to describe a specific type of instinctive response resulting from childhood abuse and complex trauma.

In his discussion on 'fawning', Walker asserts that trauma-based codependency is learned very early in life when a child gives up protesting abuse to avoid parental retaliation, thereby relinquishing the ability to say "no" and behave assertively. This also results in the *repression* of the trauma–associated 'fight' response (2003).

How to Tell If You're a 'Fawner'

'Fawners' are typically individuals who were raised in a dysfunctional or abusive family system and were 'trained' by their primary caregivers to repress and deny their feelings, thoughts, and needs. Such children learn early on in life that their true self-expressions and natural impulses are not acceptable to those they depend on for survival and that their self-worth must be extracted from those around them in a never-ending quest to feel 'okay', accepted, valued, and loved.

A healthy adult relationship requires that the two people involved create a relational environment that is reciprocal, truthful, respectful, and interdependent. However, if you're a 'fawner', (also referred to at times as *people-pleaser* or *codependent*), you likely seek validation from others that you are acceptable and worthy of being liked or loved. You can be so 'other' focused and 'enmeshed' that you may have no idea what you actually feel, think, want, or need.

If you identify as being a 'fawner', you may be engaging in people-pleasing behaviors to avoid conflict as much as possible in your interactions with others. You will deny your truth in an attempt to make those you feel dependent upon, afraid of, or care about comfortable.

As someone with a 'fawning' trauma response, you may do anything you can to 'keep the peace', even if that means abandoning yourself by repressing your preferences, thoughts, and needs, which in turn deprives you of the ability to negotiate on matters important to you, whether personal or professional.

You may be so focused on tending to the wants and needs of those around you that you have lost touch with who you are at the most basic level, to the point where you might be feeling depleted, angry, and exhausted much of the time without ever realizing it is because of your chronic, people-pleasing ways. Because you did not experience yourself as *lovable* by your primary caregivers when young, you may be intent on caretaking and helping others to prove that you are at least somewhat *valuable,* and therefore *needed.*

Why Appeasing Others Serves Nobody in the End

As you may have already discovered, engaging in subservient, ingratiating behavior that results in your feeling like a doormat isn't helpful to anyone, no matter how much you may like to believe it is – especially if you are the 'scapegoat' in your family.

By surrendering to the will of others and abandoning yourself, you are allowing yourself to live a lie – and lies serve no one in the end. This will also make you highly vulnerable to attracting narcissistic, abusive people who will exploit your willingness to deny your own feelings, wants and needs in deference to their own.

Ten Steps To Overcome 'Fawning' Behaviors

Although it takes courage to practice new behaviors, people who live authentically find that the freedom they experience in being themselves makes risking conflict worth it. The following strategies are some 'tried and true' methods I created for my *FSA Recovery Coaching* clients to help them positively transform fawning and people-pleasing behaviors so as to live a happier, more emotionally honest and fulfilled life:

1. Recognize that you may have learned early in life that your self-worth depends on what others think of you (adult survivors of child abuse, including family scapegoating abuse, are especially likely to believe this).

2. Acknowledge that your self-worth does not belong in the hands of others – Nobody should have that much power over what you think and feel about yourself.

3. Decide that you will no longer play the *'People-Pleasing Game'*. It will take time, dedication, and commitment to replace the 'fawning' response with healthier, more assertive behaviors, but it is indeed possible, and the rewards of living authentically make any conflict experienced more than worth it.

4. Check in with yourself during interactions with others, especially when communicating with those that you tend to people-please the most. Focus on what feels most true and right for you during these conversations, even if you are not yet ready to risk conflict by expressing a differing view, feeling, want, or need. Write your thoughts and feelings down in a journal after any difficult or uncomfortable interactions. Get to know yourself and become curious about what you feel and think.

5. Determining your values, priorities, and beliefs are three of the most effective ways to build a strong foundation from which to speak your truth when communicating with others. Take time to be with yourself and write down your life goals and commitments based on what is most important to you. This will help you to develop your ability to agree or disagree and say "no" or "yes" (and mean it), no matter what the situation is.

6. "My decision is final": Once you determine your values and better understand what is best and most right for you, plan on saying "My decision is final" if you anticipate that rejecting or denying a request will not be well received. Role-play with your significant other, a trusted friend, or a therapist or life coach (if needed) so you can get used to saying this one simple phrase. These four words will go a long

way to ensure that any doors that might allow you to be manipulated by others, especially people who were able to take advantage of you in the past, are firmly closed, which will save you much grief down the road. As a friend from the South once shared with me, "Be careful about letting the Devil in for tea, because next thing you know they'll stay for lunch, then dinner, and next thing you know they're moving in!"

7. Use empathic reflection when asserting yourself in your daily interactions, including recognized 'authority figures': Here's an example from my own life: I recently saw a doctor for a minor physical complaint. His recommended intervention was unacceptable to me for various reasons. My response was to say, "I understand why you might be recommending that, and if I were in your shoes I imagine I would too. But that route is not one I wish to go down. My decision is final." After saying this and dialoguing a bit more, we went on to find a remedy that we both felt comfortable with and the treatment was ultimately successful.

8. Choose your battles: If you sense or suspect that your honest expressions are going to result in a conflict that you just don't feel ready or equipped to deal with, it's okay to acknowledge this truth to yourself and choose not to express it. Some things matter

more than others. Talk to a trusted friend, journal
your thoughts and feelings, or consider seeing a
Psychotherapist, Counselor, or certified Life Coach
to help you sort out what matters most to you and
what doesn't. Remember, some people will not be
able to hear or compassionately receive, much less
respect, your truth if they find it personally or
professionally inconvenient or threatening. Not
everyone is looking for honest, reciprocal
relationships or interactions; such people may
attempt to judge, shame, or blame you for speaking
your truth, or try to convince you (or others) that
your truth is a lie.

9. Don't explain yourself in an attempt to justify your
position: This is a real trap that people-pleasing types
fall into repeatedly. You're entitled to have your own
thoughts, feelings, experiences, needs, and
preferences, just like everybody else. The fact that
some people in your life may not agree with you or
respect your truth doesn't make them right. Trust
yourself and your perceptions. Sometimes our "gut
feelings' can tell us far more about a person or
situation than anything that is being overtly
presented to us.

10. Remember the power of choice: Adults who learned
to fawn and people-please in childhood are often
genuinely unaware that they can choose how they

will conduct themselves in a relationship. If you are tired of feeling like a door-mat, then it may be time to get up off of the floor.

Living in an emotionally honest manner requires courage, patience, practice, and commitment. There are many books written on people-pleasing and codependency designed to help fawners break the people-pleasing habit. Melody Beattie's *Codependent No More: How To Stop Controlling Others And Start Caring For Yourself* is the book/workbook I most often recommend to clients, along with Susan Newman's *The Book of No: 250 Ways To Say It – And Mean It And Stop People-Pleasing Forever*. Working with a *trauma-informed* licensed Psychotherapist or certified Life Coach who understands codependency or attending a free support group such as *Al-Anon* that focuses on developing healthy relationships and communication can be very helpful as well.

Take Small Steps Every Day

Once you feel ready to begin risking conflict in your personal or professional interactions, consider choosing one person in your life that you can practice being completely honest with; ideally, this person will be someone you know to be trustworthy, caring, and emotionally safe. Then say exactly what's on your mind and see what happens. Think of your values, take deep breaths, and stand your ground. You might be pleasantly surprised to find that any fear encountered in being authentic in your relationships is temporary and that the rewards of living in an emotionally honest, integral, and values-based manner make it more than worth any temporary discomfort.

Sometimes when you speak your truth it will not go very smoothly, particularly if you're standing up to someone in your family system that has scapegoated, demeaned, or disrespected you in the past. Your honest expressions may actually incite the recipient to attack you aggressively, whether openly or covertly, and could lead to your being scapegoated even more intensely. In such situations, you may have to weigh 'risks' versus 'rewards', as outlined in item 8 (*'choose your battles'*).

A word of caution: If you believe that you are genuinely not safe in a relationship and that asserting your boundaries and speaking your truth could result in a threat to your physical safety or jeopardize your mental and emotional well-being, I urge you to contact The *National Domestic Violence Hotline* **to receive support, information, and guidance.**

Now that you have some tools to help you assert yourself and effectively communicate your feelings, thoughts, wants, and needs, we'll explore how you can use all that you have learned in this guide to release the 'scapegoat story' for good.

10

RELEASING THE 'FAMILY SCAPEGOAT' STORY

Although the work of freeing yourself from the painful and damaging role of 'family scapegoat' isn't easy, it is indeed possible to reclaim the truth of who you are so that you can live a self-empowered life that includes love, respect, serenity, and clarity. Your recovery will hinge upon one basic concept: Cultivating a connection with, and embodying, your 'true self', free of the 'shaming and blaming' family scapegoat (false) narrative.

Letting Go of False Family Narratives

When I first begin to work with clients who are suffering from the mental and emotional anguish caused by family scapegoating abuse (FSA), I help them understand that they have been imprisoned in a role common to dysfunctional/ narcissistic family systems. This highly destructive arrangement invariably benefits the power-holders in their family-of-origin (often one or both parents, but not always).

While educating my clients on FSA, I explain that their personal narrative, i.e., their unique life story, has been *co-opted and distorted* by those empowered within their family to do so as part of a macabre and complex multigenerational 'dance'. Said differently: **Their identity has become embedded within a twisted, distorted, 'shaming and blaming' narrative which acts like a cancer that metastasizes and spreads throughout the 'body' of their nuclear and extended family.**

In place of the truth of who they are, the scapegoated child/ adult child becomes imprisoned within an extraordinarily damaging false narrative that requires them to accept their 'role' as faulty, damaged, and 'bad'. If they recognize what is actually going on and protest against being 'defined and maligned' in this way, few in the family will align with them or come to their defense or aid. Assumptions and conclusions are made about their character and motivations that are typically damning, unjust, and unfair. To make matters worse, they have no way to assert their truth, as whatever they say in their own defense is unlikely to be believed due to their having been discredited and dis-empowered within their family system.

For example, one client of mine was asked by an uncle to temporarily store a family heirloom at her house as he was moving out-of-state. Apparently, one of the uncle's sisters (my client's aunt) felt she had a right to claim this particular heirloom as she believed that their long-deceased parents had meant to give it to her.

Imagine my client's surprise a few months later when she heard that her aunt believed she had "stolen" the heirloom her uncle had temporarily left in her care and wanted to call the police and turn her in for this (assumed) act of theft – yet had never reached out to my client personally to inquire about the heirloom in question and hear their side of the story.

This was a relative my client had dearly loved who had been very generous and loving to her as a child. The genuine shock she felt upon first learning she was being called a "criminal" by members of her extended family, combined with her confusion as to why this relative had not contacted her to ask why the heirloom was in her possession, was genuinely traumatizing for her and is still painful for her to think about or discuss to this day.

A Shocking Moment of Clarity

The analogy I use for describing that "Aha!" moment when

you realize you are the 'family scapegoat' is taken from the final scene of the 1995 film, "*The Usual Suspects.*" In this story about five criminals who are arrested and brought in for questioning, the entire narrative of the film relies on an unreliable narrator. As with the ending of this movie, realizing that nothing was as you believed it to be can be both devastating and dazzling, once you get over the initial confusion, outrage, and disbelief.

Realizing that the truth of ourselves has been twisted into something else (something we do not relate to or identify with), we must begin re-constructing the actual 'plot', or 'story', of our lives – A plot in which we were negatively impacted by a family projection process that co-opted our personal narrative. This process of 'uncovering and discovering' the truth of our actual position in the family is the first step toward healing and recovering from being in the 'family scapegoat' role.

The 'Gordian Knot' of Family Dysfunction

How does a person go about releasing the 'scapegoat story' in order to reclaim the truth of who they are after having their unique life story hijacked and co-opted by their family? Although there are many possible pathways for healing from the negative effects of family scapegoating abuse, one thing that *must* happen is your personal narrative, your unique life story, your sense of who you are, and the deepest truths about yourself must be *recovered, aligned with, integrated,* and *embodied* for genuine healing and transformation to take place. Said differently, **your reality, your voice, and your truth need** to be reclaimed and restored – whether your family can acknowledge and support this process or not.

Something I'm often asked by clients and readers of my articles on FSA is, "How can I heal from multigenerational dysfunction and abuse if those family members who are scapegoating me are not willing to look at their damaging behaviors and actions?" When considering this, I like to use the analogy of the 'Gordian knot' to describe the process of recovering from family scapegoating abuse (FSA) and child abuse in general.

The term *"Gordian knot"* describes a complex or unsolvable problem or puzzle and is based on an event in the life of *Alexander the Great.*

In 333 B.C. Alexander the Great encountered an ancient wagon with its yoke tied with several seemingly impossibly tangled knots.

It seemed that the wagon had once belonged to Gordius, the father of King Midas. An oracle had declared that anyone who could untie the knots was destined to become ruler of all of Asia.

Upon learning this, Alexander immediately began wrestling with the knots, without success. After pronouncing that it made no difference how the knots were untangled, he drew out his sword and sliced the knot in half in one single stroke.

Recovering from family scapegoating abuse requires a similar, efficient, 'slicing-through' process. Whether or not we 'cut off' contact with certain family members will depend on many factors (including cultural and financial considerations and the degree of maltreatment/abuse); however, going 'no contact' is not the sort of 'slicing through' that I'm talking about. Instead, I encourage clients to consider the possibility that they can **dis-identify** from the 'shaming and blaming' stories directed at them via *'slicing through' to the truth of who they actually are.*

This is why releasing the 'scapegoat story' created by your parent(s) or other family members is a critical component of recovering from the betrayal trauma associated with family scapegoating abuse. **Remember, this is just their story about you – their distorted, one-dimensional version of reality – and their portrayal of you likely has little to do with who you actually are.**

While none of us are perfect and family members can certainly have their differences and engage in conflict, calling someone "mentally" or "emotionally ill," a "fake," a "liar", or "a thief" as a means of establishing interpersonal dominance is not only inappropriate, **but is in fact a form of bullying and psycho-emotional abuse.** Nobody has the right to malign and define you or determine your value or worth, much less slander you to your face or behind your back, including (and especially) your family.

An Attitude of 'Radical Acceptance'

Full recovery also requires an attitude of 'radical acceptance': Life is not fair, and bad things happen to good people. How do we as FSA survivors radically accept what happened to us and the losses we incurred, including in some cases lost family connections and damage to our personal or professional reputations? How do we feel 'whole' when the injustices, betrayals, and losses we experienced are severe and for the most part go unacknowledged and unrecognized?

My experience is that allowing yourself to move through the stages that lead to 'radical acceptance' with the support of someone who understands, such as a knowledgeable therapist or trauma-informed recovery coach, is a key aspect of recovering from FSA, particularly as related to moving through the stages of *denial, anger, bargaining,* and *complicated/ disenfranchised grief,* as discussed in an earlier chapter. We also need to release the false, shamed self so as to realign with our 'true self' nature.

In the following chapter, I review how children raised in dysfunctional families develop a 'false self' in order to experience a sense of attachment, connection, and belonging. Embedded within this 'false self' may be the belief that they are fundamentally flawed or 'bad'. This is especially true for the scapegoated child.

11

THE DEVELOPMENT OF THE FALSE SELF

While repressing core parts of ourselves that are deemed unacceptable by those caring for us may be necessary for our survival while we are dependent children, this can contribute to a variety of mental and emotional difficulties, both in childhood and as an adult, that may eventually need to be examined and addressed in therapy. Scapegoated children in particular may become so thoroughly identified with a 'shamed and blamed' false self that they feel inherently flawed, damaged, and unworthy of love at the unconscious level.

Childhood Attachment and the False Self

As a *transpersonally-oriented* therapist, I place great emphasis on examining egoic-driven '*maladaptive survival responses*' (i.e., survival coping behaviors) learned in childhood, as it is these foundational responses/behaviors that most often result in dysfunctional attachment patterns and inhibit the expression of our *true self* (also referred to as the '*real self*', *authentic self*, or the '*intrinsic self*') as adults.

Given this, I invariably invite my FSA recovery clients to explore how such survival response patterns (which can include *trauma responses*) might have resulted in their living from a 'false self' versus their authentic center. We can then also explore how these maladaptive coping behaviors learned in childhood might be contributing to their mental and emotional distress and negatively impacting their relationships today.

This process of denying and repressing our 'true self' is largely unconscious – **Somehow we innately 'know' as children of dysfunctional, emotionally immature, or personality disordered parents that our most full and vibrant self cannot be tolerated within our family system.** We fear losing connection with those we depend upon for our emotional and physical survival, and so we succumb to the 'rules' that demand we become silent, accepting, and accommodating.

Because attachment to others is a critical aspect of our childhood development, the healthy formation of our egoic/socialized self depends upon it. We learn early on in life that we must appease our primary caregiver(s) at all cost; as a consequence, we morph and reshape ourselves into what we are expected (or demanded) by them to be.

It should be noted that this process of becoming disconnected from the *true self* in response to a non-accepting, non-approving, and non-nurturing family environment allows the child to mentally and emotionally survive within their family-of-origin, but is considered to be maladaptive as the child grows older in that these coping behaviors interfere with healthy adult functioning and relating.

In this manner, a *false self* (which includes the 'idealized' or 'shamed/humiliated' self) develops, and we become alienated from our true self. This is especially the case if we are feeling threatened or unsafe; thus it is common for children who grew up in dysfunctional/toxic/abusive home environments to live nearly entirely as a false self when they become adults, with all of the negative consequences (e.g., addiction, codependency, depression, anxiety, self-esteem issues, unstable relationships, etc).

As mentioned in Chapter 8, my FSA research suggests that if the rejected, shamed, or bullied child is an empath or highly sensitive person (HSP), they will typically fall into the role of 'caretaker', 'helper', or 'parentified child', in addition to possibly becoming the 'family scapegoat'. **Because they do not feel inherently *lovable*, they instead seek to be viewed as '*valuable*'** by becoming a source of support and care for their parent(s) and perhaps other nuclear (or extended) family members, such as siblings. Such children often become the 'emotional caretaker' and 'feeler' for their family, and are likely to develop the 'fawning' trauma response, as mentioned.

The Suppression of the True Self

In a sense, an unspoken, unconscious agreement is made in the child's quest for acceptance, connection, attachment, and love: *"If I become what you want and need me to be, you will then love me and not abandon me or reject me."* The true self is suppressed and hidden as the child learns how they must behave, think, and express themselves in order to fit in and experience a sense of belonging and acceptance. But this artificial harmony comes at great cost to the child, who has lost access to their enlivened, natural self and 'felt-sense' experience. Adaptive survival responses also can result in the child repeatedly finding themselves in dysfunctional, toxic, or abusive relationships when they become an adult.

Alternatively, if we as children don't adapt and 'go along to get along', i.e, if we choose authenticity over attachment and rebel against the restrictions placed on us by the power-holders in our family-of-origin, we can be seen as emotionally or mentally unstable, dangerous, and threatening, as well as "angry," "different," "difficult," "needy," "selfish," "cold," "unloving," "narcissistic," "unreasonable," etc.

When being authentic results in our being scapegoated by our family in this way, we are caught in a 'double bind', i.e., the 'Gordian knot' I spoke of earlier, meaning we are "damned if we do" and "damned if we don't", which makes choosing authenticity over artifice a challenge. Whether they choose to play the role the family is comfortable with, or whether they choose to rebel, the scapegoated child will experience intrapsychic pain and conflict either way. If later the (now adult) child consciously decides to live and act authentically at some point, it may be intolerable to a highly dysfunctional family, *for what the system cannot control or accept, it will reject and eject.*

Ultimately, the adult child in such a situation must decide if they will sacrifice their truth to ease tensions within their family, or remain authentic and suffer the consequence of lost connection and attachment within their family system – a system that is unable to tolerate the totality of who and what they are (something I see frequently with my 'celebrity' clients and clients that have achieved other obvious forms of professional or personal success).

Maladaptive Responses and the Primal Wound

It should be noted that the impulse to shape and socialize a child and quell their natural, creative expression is rarely *consciously* chosen by the parent; rather, it is most often an *unconscious reaction*. Meaning, it is an *automatic response*, versus being conscious and intentional on the parent's part.

Often the parent is re-enacting their past by projecting their process of lost authenticity onto their children, repeating a pattern that has likely been passed down for generations. Like it or not, our childhood attachment styles and maladaptive survival responses on some level determine our fate. This is because these survival responses, when they overpower our authentic nature, become an *unconscious blueprint* for how we will or will not connect and attach in our primary relationships – especially our most intimate ones.

It is therefore critical that the adult survivor of childhood abuse becomes aware of this core intrapsychic *primal wound* that developed in response to their shaming and rejecting environment, as it is this core wound that is fueling much of their psychological and emotional difficulties and interpersonal distress.

This is why I view recovering from family scapegoating abuse as being a **process of reclamation** whereby we *discover, recover, and reclaim* the true self lost in childhood. As we examine ourselves to see who we are and who we are not, we eventually can identify the survival responses that no longer serve us as adults, while at the same time releasing all that is false and survival-based. In this way, we can live from our center, confident within the truth of our being, free of distorted, self-negating narratives.

Existing as our true self within this innate and natural 'Ground of Being', we may at last stand on a firm inner foundation of 'Self-hood', versus the cracked and shaking inner ground inherited from our dysfunctional family system. It is from this place of deep, inner connection and constancy that we can create a rich and soulful (*soul-filled*) life, one that is nourished by a sense of inner passion and purpose, free of the 'scapegoat' identity.

Next, I'll be sharing ten strategies for recovering and embodying the true self that are designed to help you dis-identify from external and internal 'shaming and blaming' narratives.

12

RECOVERING THE TRUE SELF LOST IN CHILDHOOD

In addition to releasing the negative, shaming and blaming 'scapegoat story' that underpins all family scapegoating dynamics, making a conscious decision to align with and live as your 'true self' is another critical aspect of recovering from this particularly egregious form of systemic dysfunction and abuse.

Reconnecting With Your True Self

When you can recognize and embody the truth of who you are and live from a place of integrity, it is easier to dis-identify from distorted family narratives. From this place of mindful awareness, it becomes possible to see that the stories you have been burdened with – sometimes for decades – are nothing more than illusory egoic-driven 'reality constructs' that bear little relation to your person or character.

Although living as one's true self might seem like a natural thing to do, those of us who grew up in a family system that did not support our uninhibited and natural expressions may have gradually disconnected from the truth of our being, i.e., our essence, so as to be accepted by those we were dependent upon to meet our physical and emotional needs.

Uncovering and embodying your truth is a critically important aspect of recovering from family scapegoating abuse (FSA). To 'reclaim' means *to retrieve, redeem, recover, return to, reform, recall, to cultivate, to cry out against, to tame, to save.* If you are trapped in the role of 'family scapegoat', you will be required to do all of these things – and more – as part of your recovery and healing process, beginning with the decision to release the 'scapegoat story' and become the author of your own life, free of the dehumanizing narratives created by members of your nuclear or extended family.

One of the most powerful healing tools available to FSA

survivors seeking to shed the false 'scapegoat' narrative is sharing the truth of what happened to them with sympathetic and supportive others. This can be done in well-facilitated 'adult survivor' recovery forums or via working with a qualified (and trauma-informed) psychotherapist, counselor, or coach, one who understands the damaging nature of being in the 'family scapegoat' role.

As mentioned earlier, I find as a clinician that using a *trauma-informed approach* incorporating **SAMHSA's** (*safety; trustworthiness and transparency; peer support; collaboration and mutuality; empowerment, voice and choice; and cultural issues*) is especially important because it has been my experience that adults who were (and perhaps still are) targets of family scapegoating often exhibit symptoms of Complex post-traumatic stress disorder (C-PTSD) due to having been chronically maltreated by one or more family members as children (and who may still be suffering in the 'scapegoat' role as adults).

How to Live and Speak Your Truth

If I were to ask you right now, "In what situations, or around which people, do you feel most yourself, and most creative, free, and alive," what would your answer be? Alternatively, if I were to ask you, "In what situations, or around which people, do you *not* feel like your authentic/true self and *less than* who and what you sense yourself to be," how might you respond?

Contemplating these two questions can be provocative, to say the least, and there may be no obvious answers at first.

If you feel ready to shed everything about yourself that feels false so as to live from a place of emotional honesty, personal integrity (inspired by your principles and values), and direct knowledge of Self, the following strategies I designed to assist my psychotherapy and coaching clients can aid you in this courageous quest.

Strategies for True-Self Cultivation

The ten strategies listed here will help you cultivate the ability to live and speak your truth from a place of positive self-regard and personal integrity. If you are not already seeing a competent therapist, counselor, or coach who can support you in your efforts, you might consider engaging such services before implementing the following suggestions:

1. *Recognize You Have a* **True Self** *Nature*: Each of us enters the world possessing an innate, core, true self. Each one of us is an 'original model', and as such we all have unique gifts to offer to the world.

2. *Remember and Reflect on When You Felt Happiest as a Child*: Think back to when you were young. When did you feel most free, happy, and alive? Take a few minutes after reflecting on what caused you to feel joyful in your youth, going back to your earliest conscious memory. Then write about the people, places, things, and activities that brought you a sense of pleasure, contentment, and satisfaction while you were growing up. This simple 'remembering and reflection' exercise can assist us in reconnecting with the innocent purity of our authentic, true self.

3. *Make a Commitment to Recover the Innately Pure, Authentic Essence Within*: In a certain sense, recognizing and consciously reclaiming our unique,

'true self' is a paradoxical process of finding and embracing what we never really lost. It is an excavation project, of sorts, i.e., it is a process of uncovering, discovering, recovering, and consciously reclaiming who (and what) we have always been, and will always be – that which is most real, honest, expansive, and alive within ourselves, yet constant and unchanging: Our true self nature.

4. *Make a Decision to Release All That Feels False and No Longer Serves You*: Becoming authentic and emotionally honest requires that we be willing to release the parts of ourselves that we were conditioned to become by the various social systems we have been immersed within like a fish swimming in the sea – from our family-of-origin to the cultural and social systems we currently identify with, and everything in between. Ask yourself if you feel ready to begin doing that. If not, I encourage you to explore what might be inhibiting you from living an emotionally honest and authentic life. Change is never easy. It's never too late to "get real". As the Indian mystic Ramana Maharshi once said, *"Let what comes, come. Let what goes, go. See what remains."*

5. *The Process of Letting Go*: I often ask my clients who are engaged in a process of *true self* recovery and reclamation, "Is this (person, place, thing, behavior, situation) serving you at the *highest level* today?"

Whatever is not serving us at the highest level is more than likely not serving others in our life at the highest level either, regardless of how it may seem. It ultimately benefits no one when we allow ourselves to tolerate abusive behavior, remain small, diminish our internal light, and hide our truth from others (and perhaps even from ourselves).

6. *The Only Way Out is Through*: It is often during this process of letting go of what feels false that long-buried emotions unconsciously repressed in childhood may surface, resulting in our possibly becoming sad, anxious, angry, or clinically depressed. At times such as this, it is imperative that a person feels that they are not alone in the valiant task of facing any painful feelings and memories that may arise head-on, versus avoiding the challenging, difficult work of genuine transformational growth. Therefore, this is a time when the help of a trusted therapist, counselor, transformational life coach, or a peer-support group such as *Al-Anon* can prove to be invaluable to a person engaged in the task of reclaiming and embodying their true self.

7. *It's Okay to Experience and Release Old, Pent-Up Feelings From Childhood*: It is also not uncommon for a person who was rejected, shamed, blamed, neglected, or otherwise mistreated in childhood to find they are experiencing feelings of intense anger –

even rage – during this critical time of transformation fueled by deep self-exploration and intrapsychic excavation. This can especially surprise those who strove to be 'nice' their entire lives to avoid upsetting others and risking conflict. I like to remind my clients during such times that the word 'courage' includes the word 'rage', and successful passage through what might feel like a *dark night of the soul* is ultimately brought about by processing these more difficult feelings and emotions that society labels as being 'negative'. Those who were victims of neglect or other forms of abuse in childhood are especially prone to finding themselves overwhelmed with these darker, extremely intense feelings; thus, working with a licensed psychotherapist or joining an abuse recovery network such as *Adult Survivors of Child Abuse* can be especially critical during this phase of personal recovery, healing, and growth. Finding resources that are specifically trauma-informed are also helpful, such *Roland Bal's* trauma-informed meditation website (search on 'Roland Bal' and 'trauma-informed meditation' to find online).

8. *Pay Attention to Your Dreams*: I have also learned from both personal and professional experience that this is a time to pay attention to one's active imagination, dreams, and fantasies, as suggested by

the great Swiss psychologist Carl Jung, for these signs and symbols emanating from deep within our unconscious invariably reveal important keys to a given individual's growth and may act as an inner 'wise guide' once one understands how to go about interpreting the personal and universal symbols contained therein. A book that I often recommend to clients for such insight-oriented dream work is Jeremy Taylor's *Dream Work: Techniques for Discovering the Creative Power in Dreams.*

9. *Release the Limiting Views of Others:* This is also a time when a person might report to their therapist, coach, or support network that they are feeling increasingly uncomfortable around family members, colleagues, and friends if those relationships were dependent on their being a certain way — a way that no longer feels integral or true (if it ever did). This is especially the case when one has knowingly or unknowingly been playing out a particular role within a given relationship or system (e.g., hero, rescuer, 'black sheep', enabler) or been an unwitting recipient of another's psychological projections (a process whereby humans defend themselves against their unpleasant impulses by denying their existence while attributing them to others). At some point, you may have no choice other than to make it clear that you are no longer willing to distort or hide your true

self to protect or appease others, and that you simply will not accept being manipulated into living out limiting, damaging role(s) as mandated by your dysfunctional family's 'script' so that the status quo (aka *homeostasis*) can be maintained.

10. *You're Not Obligated to Play by Other People's Rules*: If it wasn't clear before, once you commit to living your life in an integral, authentic, connected manner it will quickly become evident that every system has its 'rules', be it a family system, a work system, a political system, etc. **This is a good time to remember that whatever the system can't change, control, or accept, it will attempt to diminish, label, reject, and (in extreme cases) 'eject'.** Be prepared to make some tough choices if this happens, such as decisions around the amount of contact you'll have with family, both nuclear and extended.

These ten strategies are designed to help you mindfully cultivate the ability to act and live as your true self. Practicing these strategies will likely not feel natural or easy at first, especially if you are an empath-type or your trauma response to conflict is 'fawning' – and as such may be especially difficult initially for survivors of FSA.

This is why I see every person who is engaged in a sincere process of *true self recovery and reclamation* as being heroic, for it is no easy task to realize and embody the truth of who and what you are while attempting to maintain relationships with others who may be demanding you "change back" (whether overtly or covertly) so that they might feel more comfortable, in control, and secure. However, with time, practice, and patience, you'll find it becomes easier to remain 'true to your true self' and not feel impacted or thrown off-center by the negative narratives imposed upon you by others – including your family-of-origin.

With that said, if the scapegoating behaviors directed toward you are severe, you may have no choice but to consider limiting or ending contact with family members who continue to subject you to hostile or abusive acts designed to demean, shame, blame, control, or ostracize you.

One way that FSA recovery can be sabotaged is via the unconscious experience of toxic shame. In the next chapter, I'll describe toxic shame and why it can be an impediment to realigning with one's true self.

13

HOW 'TOXIC SHAME' INTERFERES WITH RECOVERY

Sometimes we can feel 'stuck' in our recovery from childhood wounding and dysfunctional family dynamics. Often this is due to something called 'toxic shame'. Understanding toxic shame can help you avoid falling back into adaptive survival response patterns and assist you in remaining connected to your true self.

The Only Way Out Is Through

When clients who are new to my practice report that they have a history of sabotaging their recovery efforts despite their sincere desire to heal, or have a strong inner critic or feel like an impostor in their personal or professional life, I let them know that 'toxic shame' may be at the root of their difficulties.

There will usually be a lot of questions about what toxic shame is, and what makes it different from 'regular' or 'ordinary' shame (i.e., shame caused by something that we have done or thought that we rightly feel guilty about or regret).

Toxic shame is a result of growing up in an environment that failed to support our developing selves as children. Ultimately, it is a failure of being empathically held and contained within our 'original tribe': Our family system.

When children grow up in environments where they are viewed in a negative light and are made to feel that they are inadequate, a failure, "stupid," incompetent, or defective in some way, they are likely to see themselves as being unworthy of love and the cause of their parent's rejection. This leads to the development of a sense of deep 'core shame' that is chronic and pervasive, but unconscious. This is commonly referred to in recovery literature as *toxic shame*.

Children believe what the adults around them say – their primary caregivers (typically the parents), especially. If a parent/

caregiver tells the child they are "worthless," "difficult," "a problem," "dumb," "lazy," "ugly," etc, the child is very likely to believe these things and the damage caused could negatively impact them life-long without successful intervention and treatment.

Specifically: When the primary caregiver behaves in ways that feel rejecting to the child (as with family scapegoating abuse), they will see themselves as the cause of their own rejection, with the root unconscious belief being "I am not lovable, there must be something wrong with me." And because the child internalizes the negative voices around them, they will eventually talk to themselves in the same negative manner that the scapegoating parent (or sibling, etc.) did.

How Toxic Shame Differs From Ordinary Shame

Toxic shame is chronic and those who suffer from it are not consciously aware that they are suffering from deeply embedded unconscious shame. It exists 'on the back burner' of our psyche, causing havoc, and yet we do not even know it is there. It is nearly always rooted in childhood and is directly connected to 'shaming stories' about ourselves that were imprinted on us when young – typically by our primary caregivers (but not always).

Toxic shame also causes 'shame anxiety' (i.e., the fear of being shamed), and the resulting 'shame spirals' can be intense and affect one physically. The heart may race, the face flush, and the extreme anxiety experienced can lead to a panic attack. Toxic shame is also closely related to 'toxic guilt', whereby we feel a sense of unjust responsibility over events we actually had no control over.

Toxic shame may cause an individual to feel that they are defective and not worthy of love and respect. In severe cases involving complex trauma, they may feel that they are not good or worthy enough to exist, resulting in the experience of frequent suicidal ideation, or, in the worst of cases, actual suicide.

Toxic shame can also result in dissociation, which is a sense of not being present or not feeling connected to one's own thoughts, memories, body, and surroundings – an experience that is also a hallmark symptom of complex trauma.

As they mature, the child will learn to avoid experiencing the pain of toxic shame in a variety of ways:

1. They may continue to negate and attack themselves ("I'm worthless"; "I'm stupid"; "I'm unlovable"; "It's all my fault"; etc) and struggle with anxiety, depression, and feelings of hopelessness, despair, and futility.

2. They may avoid their inner reality via becoming what they believe other people need them to be (codependency), or attempt to escape painful inner and outer realities altogether via addiction (alcohol,

drugs, porn, shopping, work, etc.).

3. They may see themselves as a perennial victim and blame, attack, and criticize others, or become a bully themselves as they seek to dominate and overpower others in an attempt to avoid feeling as helpless and powerless as they did in childhood.

4. They may isolate themselves from others by avoiding social situations due to anxiety, a sense of mistrust, or feelings of inadequacy and incompetence. They then feel lonely but don't know how to break the pattern of isolation, which can result in feelings of frustration, anger, and helplessness.

Healing Toxic Shame

Something I often say to clients is that we must start by learning to tune into the subtle (or not so subtle) signals emanating from our bodies, as well as pay attention to our internal dialogue (things we say to ourselves about ourselves and others). This requires bringing yourself into the present moment – something people who experience toxic shame and complex trauma tend to avoid as it can be painful and uncomfortable to sit with their own experiences, thoughts, and feelings.

Eventually, you will be able to identify *negative automatic thoughts* you have about yourself or others. Once you notice, take a big breath and then imagine that thought rolling out of your mind down a beautiful green hill into a boat on a river.

The boat then drifts off and carries all of your negative, critical, shaming thoughts away.

You might also become aware of bodily symptoms indicating toxic shame before you begin to notice your thoughts. Perhaps your face turns red and you feel hot; or your heart begins to race; or you suddenly feel overwhelmed, frightened, fatigued, tired, anxious, or depressed. These might all be symptoms of repressed emotions, including toxic shame.

Healing toxic shame requires being able to forge non-judging, non-shaming, accepting relationships with others in an emotionally safe environment. For some, this means reaching out to a trauma-informed therapist who understands toxic shame, childhood abuse, and family systems issues, or working with a similarly qualified professional who understands issues specific to adult survivors of child abuse.

In the next chapter, I'll explore the unique challenges adult survivors face when recovering from family scapegoating abuse.

14

UNIQUE CHALLENGES OF FSA RECOVERY

Individuals intent on releasing the 'scapegoat story' for good face unique challenges in regard to their recovery. For example, if their family is unable to see them as a 'whole' person and continues to place them in the 'family scapegoat' role, some difficult decisions will need to be made in order to establish and protect their own mental and emotional well-being.

Family System Dysfunction and Homeostasis

My clinical experiences working with families in psychiatric inpatient and addiction treatment settings, along with my FSA research findings, suggest that family members who scapegoat one of their own are typically unable or unwilling to acknowledge how their harmful actions and words have negatively impacted the target of their behavior. They are also likely to resist invitations to address the issue in a therapeutic setting.

For example, if the scapegoated family member has become dependent on drugs or alcohol as a means of escaping their psycho-emotional pain and enters a treatment center, they may be mandated to participate in some type of family therapy as part of their care plan; however, this does not mean that their position as 'family scapegoat' will be recognized and effectively addressed, including by their treatment provider (such as their case manager or assigned therapist).

In rare instances when the scapegoating family member(s) do agree to meet in a family therapy setting with the FSA survivor, their egoic defenses will make them intractable in their position that they are 'right' and that the scapegoated family member is the 'offender' (this is especially true when the scapegoated family member is known to be an alcoholic/addict or has a history of psychiatric hospitalization). They might also claim that *they* are the victim, denying their hurtful behaviors altogether, thereby victimizing the scapegoated family member twice. This strategic defense maneuver is known as <u>DARVO</u>, which stands for **"Deny, Attack, and Reverse Victim and Offender"** (Freyd, J.J. 1997).

This is especially the case in families where there are 'secrets', such as sexual/physical abuse of the scapegoated child. Because such families are unlikely to seek out counseling of their own accord, it is invariably the family 'identified patient' (i.e., the victim of family scapegoating abuse) who eventually reaches out for some type of Mental Health assistance to address their psycho-emotional distress. Hence, this guide has focused on what the FSA survivor can do to help themselves achieve a sense of well-being and intrapsychic wholeness, *independent of their family-of-origin dynamics changing*.

"Change Back!" (Reject/Eject)

Remember, what the system cannot control, it will very often attempt to reject and 'eject'. I often discuss 'crab theory' or 'crab mentality' with my clients to explain this confusing aspect of dysfunctional family systems: Specifically, as a crab is trying to climb out of the bucket it is trapped in as part of the day's catch, **other crabs will do their utmost to pull it back down into the bucket, ruining its chance of escape.** This is often how it is when you are trying to recover from the effects of being raised in a dysfunctional family system. **As you become more able to exist as your true self, your**

family system will be challenged to accommodate and accept the healthier and more functional self you are becoming.

Dysfunctional Families Are Inflexible Systems

A reasonably healthy family system can make needed adjustments to allow for personal, individual growth; however, a dysfunctional family system rarely can. Instead, the recovering adult survivor is pressured in various ways to *change back* to who and what the family is comfortable with and 'knows'. However, most healthy adults do not want to be who they were in their childhood just to make their family comfortable, especially if their role in the family was that of 'scapegoat' or they had to behave in a subordinate manner to protect themselves and survive. This is especially the case in families where the system 'power-holder' (e.g., a parent) has a personality disorder such as *Borderline* or *Narcissistic Personality Disorder* (as mentioned in the introduction) and fear their aggressive/abusive behaviors toward their now-adult child **will be revealed to other family members or publicly exposed** if conversations become more open, honest, and authentic.

Recovering From Family Scapegoating Abuse (FSA)

When an adult survivor of family scapegoating abuse first seeks out psychotherapy, they often have no idea that they grew up in a toxic, highly dysfunctional family system. They will typically present in therapy with feelings of extreme confusion, anxiety, sadness, rage, and unrecognized symptoms of complex trauma (C–PTSD).

FSA recovery therefore begins with psycho-education regarding the negative impact of growing up in an environment rife with 'invisible' or covert abuse and the traumatizing effect this may have had on their psyche, possibly from a very early age.

Identifying *maladaptive survival responses* plays a critical part in recovering from family scapegoating abuse. Maladaptive survival responses are unconscious coping mechanisms that allowed the scapegoated child to adapt to their abusive family environment, but do not serve the adult survivor well today. For example, appeasing behaviors that helped the scapegoated child to avoid the wrath of their dysfunctional or narcissistic parent might actually be the trauma response of *fawning* (as discussed in chapter nine). Such maladaptive survival and trauma responses need to be addressed as part of a *trauma-informed* therapy and recovery process.

While the adult survivor of family scapegoating abuse comes to terms with the mental and emotional damage done to them, strong – and perhaps overwhelming – emotions will invariably begin to reveal themselves. Each wave of pain, grief, and rage must be compassionately attended to as the numbness of living in a chronic state of survival or denial recedes and awareness and clarity take hold.

Missed or delayed developmental tasks (such as those that promote healthy individuation, confidence, and the ability to attach securely to others) will also need to be explored. The FSA survivor may struggle with basic self-care due to having their own needs minimized by a parent growing up, and this will also need to be assessed and addressed.

Radical Acceptance and FSA Recovery

In the later stages of family scapegoating abuse (FSA) recovery, the adult survivor may reach a state of 'radical acceptance', whereby they are able to acknowledge the many twisted and unfair things that happened to them as a result of being scapegoated in their dysfunctional family system from a place of self-compassion and self-love.

Radical acceptance is a distress tolerance skill used in Dialectical Behavioral Therapy (DBT) that is designed to prevent pain from turning into prolonged suffering. Life is not fair, and bad things happen to good people. Many feelings will arise in relation to the scapegoated adult survivor recognizing what actually happened to them in their dysfunctional family system. Over time, as these feelings are thoroughly explored and processed, the ability to 'radically accept' even the most painful realities often develops.

For the FSA adult survivor, radical acceptance does not mean that they approve of, condone, or agree with something that has happened to them that feels wrong,

undeserved, unjust, or unfair. It simply means that they acknowledge and accept that they are unable to alter, fix, or change what has happened to them in the past, nor can they 'fix' or control the harmful behaviors or actions of other people in the present, including the behaviors and actions of those in their family who may still be scapegoating them.

No longer exhausting themselves mentally and emotionally by wrestling with an unalterable past and an intolerable present, a significant amount of intrapsychic energy is freed up that can be used to make meaningful change that promotes and supports the adult FSA survivor's recovery process as they work to heal from the damage caused by being the target of family scapegoating abuse (FSA). This may include making some extremely difficult decisions, such as ending contact with nuclear or extended family members who continue to scapegoat and abuse them.

Healing Modalities and FSA Recovery

Based on responses to the *FSA Survey* I conducted as part of my research, trauma-informed psychotherapy and treatment such as *Cognitive Process Therapy* and *EMDR* or somatic-based therapies such as the *Hakomi Method* can be very helpful for the FSA adult survivor who suffers from complex trauma (C-PTSD). *Narrative Therapy, Acceptance and Commitment Therapy (ACT)*; and *Compassion-Focused Therapy (CFT)* offer evidence-based pathways for deep healing and integration. *Internal Family*

Systems therapy (IFS) is especially helpful for those who are having trouble resolving family-of-origin issues. *Psychosynthesis* can assist in increasing awareness of a deeper identity beyond the 'false' (wounded) self.

For families that are willing to see a therapist, it is important to ensure the clinician is well-versed in **Family Systems theory and practices**, such as a *Marriage, Family Therapist (MFT)*, as well as **trauma-informed** in their approach (if possible). Coaches who are certified in trauma-informed recovery approaches may also be able to help the FSA survivor. **It is also critically important that family therapy is not initiated until the abuse of the scapegoated adult survivor has stopped (I say more about this in the *Afterword*).**

Forums and social media venues that allow the FSA adult survivor to process feelings and receive support can also be helpful, such as *Adult Survivors of Child Abuse* or online communities that focus on recovering from C-PTSD, such as the online forum *Out of the Storm*.

You can find additional recovery and book recommendations in the 'Afterword' and 'Resource' sections in the back matter of this book. You are also invited to visit my website (scapegoatrecovery.com) where you can subscribe to my blog to receive my latest articles. Be sure to check out the **10 Self-Care Tips for FSA Survivors** *via my website's menu.*

Afterword

If you found this introductory guide helpful and resonated strongly with it, I encourage you to do all you can to find support and assistance to aid your FSA recovery journey so that you might give yourself the gift of a life that is free from all forms of abuse.

Given the fact that most adult survivors of family scapegoating abuse also suffer from complex trauma (C-PTSD) symptoms, it is recommended that you engage with **trauma-informed practitioners** who can competently assess you and guide you through the healing process. Many therapists and coaches are working online now, and some offer low-fee slots to those who are in financial need. Psychology Today's website allows you to use filters to find therapists in your area who address your specific issues and you can filter for online service providers as well. Click on the filter 'Types of Therapy', then 'Show More Types of Therapy' and then 'Family Systems' to find a therapist who will be familiar with family roles such as 'identified patient' and 'family scapegoat'.

Mental Health telehealth platforms like Betterhelp also offer financial aid. When you get assigned to a therapist, ask if they have expertise in family systems and whether or not they consider themselves to be *trauma-informed*.

A word of caution: I'm often asked by clients and readers of my articles if they should participate in family therapy if someone in their family suggests it. My answer? Not if the people who want you to join them in family therapy sessions are still abusing you.

Remember, if you are the 'identified patient' in your family, your truth and your experience of being scapegoated is likely to be overwhelmed by the 'stories' and negative narrative your family has about you, which they will be more than happy to share with the family therapist. When it comes to abuse, it is critical to remember that there is only truth, and what actually happened is what matters – not your family's story about you and what you supposedly did to 'deserve' less than humane treatment.

For example, if there are people in your family who claim you are "a liar"; "crazy"; "a fake"; etc, when you are none of these things, they will be quite comfortable – also eager – to tell the Family Therapist these same things with you right there in the room with them, which is understandably re-traumatizing for victims of FSA. On the other hand, if specific family members are no longer abusing you and seem sincerely open and willing to participate in family therapy so as to make amends and work toward reconciliation, then working with a highly skilled, trauma-informed *Family Systems* therapist might indeed be helpful, should you wish to remain connected with them.

Sadly, there are some Mental Health professionals who are unable to hold parents, siblings, or other relatives accountable for their abusive behaviors. We especially don't like to think that a mother or a father would harm their child, whether intentionally or unintentionally. When victims of abuse sense that their reports of family maltreatment are minimized or invalidated by the therapist, it can be a devastating experience that causes them to fear ever reaching out for help again. This is why it is critical that any therapist or recovery coach you engage with be trauma-informed and familiar with family scapegoating dynamics and the harms that such dysfunctional, toxic dynamics can cause.

Confronting any type of toxic family abuse and facing the reality that you may need to end relations with family members who persist in maltreating you is no easy task, which is why support from a competent professional who specializes in **child abuse** and **adult survivor recovery** is so very critical. As anyone who's been chronically scapegoated by family will tell you, recovering from this particular form of systemic, insidious abuse is difficult to do alone or only with the help of an online forum or self-help book, especially if C-PTSD symptoms are present.

If you strongly related to the contents of this book, I urge you to get help from a licensed or certified professional, and don't stop until you do. **For more self-care tips that have worked well for many of my FSA Recovery Coaching clients, read my article, 10 Self-Care Tips for Adult Survivors of Family Scapegoating. It is available in the menu at** *scapegoatrecovery.com.*

Additional resources are listed after the 'References' page.

References

Cloitre M., Garvert D. W., Brewin C. R., Bryant R. A., & Maercker A. (2013). Evidence for proposed ICD-11 PTSD and complex PTSD: A latent profile analysis. European Journal of Psychotraumatology, 4, 2070

DePrince, A. P. & Freyd, J. J. (2002a). The harm of trauma: Pathological fear, shattered assumptions or betrayal? J. Kauffman (Ed.) Loss of the Assumptive World (pp. 71-82).

Doka, K. J. (Ed.). (1989). Disenfranchised grief: Recognizing hidden sorrow. Lexington, MA: Lexington.

Freyd, J.J. (1997). Violations of power, adaptive blindness, and betrayal trauma theory. *Feminism & Psychology*, 7, 22-32.

Freyd, J.J. (2008). Betrayal Trauma. In G. Reyes, J.D. Elhai, & J.D.Ford (Eds) Encyclopedia of Psychological Trauma. (p. 76). New York: John Wiley & Sons.

Nidich S. et al. A randomized controlled trial on effects of the Transcendental Meditation program on blood pressure, psychological distress, and coping in young adults. Am J Hypertens. 2009 Dec;22(12):1326-31. Epub 2009 Oct 1

Walker, Pete. "Codependency, Trauma and the Fawn Response" Pete Walker, MA, MFT, Feb, 2003, www.pete-walker.com/codependencyFawnResponse.htm.

Resources

It can be difficult to find a Mental Health or other Healing Arts professional who understands the destructive and abusive aspects of family scapegoating behaviors; however, as mentioned in the last chapter of this guide, a therapist who has specific training in *Family Systems*, such as a *Licensed Marriage, Family Therapist (LMFT)*, will understand dysfunctional/narcissistic family dynamics and should be familiar with the process of helping adults free themselves from unwanted and damaging family roles. In my clinical opinion, it is also critical that the therapist is a **trauma-informed** practitioner.

Pete Walker is a United States therapist who has been writing about C-PTSD and its effects for many years and I encourage you to visit his website (www.pete-walker.com). Psychiatrist, author, and researcher *Bessel van der Kolk* wrote a 'must read' book on trauma called *The Body Keeps the Score* that discusses the neurobiology of trauma and 'rewiring' the traumatized brain. Janina Fisher's C-PTSD workbook, *Transforming the Living Legacy of Trauma*, is one that I use in my own practice with my clients, and they find it very helpful. *Peter Levine's* book, *Waking the Tiger: Healing Trauma,* is also one that my FSA recovery clients find to be very helpful. To see some of my favorite recovery books, visit my online store at *scapegoatrecovery.com.*

Online Resources

You might consider joining an online support group like *Adult Survivors of Child Abuse (ASCA)* at to connect with other adult survivors of dysfunctional/abusive families, or the *National Association of Adult Survivors of Child Abuse.* You also might try connecting with HAVOCA – *Help for Adult Victims of Child Abuse.* For a comprehensive list of organizations that help adult survivors of child abuse, visit *The Child Welfare Information Gateway.* 12-step groups like *Adult Children of Alcoholics (ACA)* and *Al-Anon* can also be very effective and phone and online meetings are available.

American spiritual teacher *Adyashanti* offers many free guided meditations that address embodying one's 'true nature' in his website's 'library' section.

Trauma-informed mindfulness practice resources are also available online for those who find most meditation practices 'triggering' or too activating. There are also trauma-informed meditation practices available online that can be explored as well. Several of my clients have benefited from *Nonviolent Communication* principles and found these to be very helpful when dealing with scapegoating family members they are still in touch with.

If you have been contemplating suicide or currently feel suicidal, please reach out to someone for help immediately. If you are in the United States, go to https://suicidepreventionlifeline.org/.

About the Author

Rebecca C. Mandeville is a licensed Marriage, Family Therapist (MFC #43860). She is a *Psychotherapist, Recovery Coach*, and recognized *Family Systems* expert who has been serving clients in clinics and in private practice for over 20 years. She served as *Core Faculty* at the world-renowned *Institute of Transpersonal Psychology*, where she first began identifying, defining, describing, and bringing attention to what she named (for research purposes) *Family Scapegoating Abuse (FSA)*.

Rebecca is also the creator of the *Family Scapegoating (FSA) Abuse Recovery Coaching* process, which was designed to help those seeking relief from the psycho-emotional distress caused by being in the 'family scapegoat' role. She writes regularly on her 'Scapegoat Recovery' blog and is a guest author for various online Mental Health organizations, including *Psych Central, Paces Connection*, and the *C-PTSD Foundation*. When not serving clients, Rebecca enjoys spending time with her partner and animals at her home on the Oregon Coast, where she finds inspiration for compassion-based, integral living.

You may write Rebecca at *contact@scapegoatrecovery.com* or visit *scapegoatrecovery.com* to learn more about her <u>FSA Recovery Coaching</u> services.

Family Scapegoating Abuse Survey

Take the FSA Survey

You may take the survey anonymously via the menu at
scapegoatrecovery.com

Permissions Statement

This publication is the copyrighted property of the author and no portion of it may be duplicated or used for non-commercial or commercial purposes without the author's express written permission. Quotes from this book that are 50 words or less may be used with proper citation.

You may email the author at **contact@scapegoatrecovery.com** *regarding permissions to use the material contained in this ebook / book.*

To learn more about Rebecca, visit her website at scapegoatrecovery.com. To discuss her participating in a media event, write her at *contact@scapegoatrecovery.com.*

Made in the USA
Middletown, DE
06 September 2024

60447980R00084